UNTYING
THE
KNOT

UNTYING THE KNOT

Protecting Your Emotional and Financial Health During Divorce

KELLY LAVALLIE CPA, CA

Copyright © 2022 by Kelly LaVallie

All rights reserved. No part of this book may be reproduced, stored in a retrieval system or transmitted, in any form or by any means, without the prior written consent of the publisher, except in the case of brief quotations, embodied in reviews and articles.

Cataloguing in publication information is available from Library and Archives Canada.
ISBN 978-1-77458-231-2 (paperback)
ISBN 978-1-77458-232-9 (ebook)

Page Two
pagetwo.com

Edited by Sarah Brohman
Cover design by Cameron McKague
Interior design by Setareh Ashrafologhalai

lavallie.ca

For my mom, who protected me from permanent damage and tried her darnedest to teach me how to spell.

Contents

Introduction *1*

ONE   PROTECTING YOUR EMOTIONAL HEALTH

1   Healthy Thinking *9*

2   Ditch Blame and Shame *27*

3   Good Behavior Gets Good Results *53*

4   Your Divorce A-Team *77*

TWO   PROTECTING YOUR FINANCIAL HEALTH

5   Managing Divorce Limbo *115*

6   Your Financial Homework *149*

7   Negotiating 101 *181*

8   The Finish Line *209*

Recommended Resources *227*

Introduction

LET ME START by saying that I'm sorry you are going through divorce or contemplating divorce. I'm a second-generation divorced person, so I feel your pain. I'd like to give you a hug, but since I'm here and you're there, instead I'm offering you heartfelt guidance in the sincere hope that it reduces your suffering.

Divorce is a common occurrence. Even though divorce rates have been falling over the last twenty years, close to a million couples are still getting divorced every year in North America alone. What's also common is that, when you ask someone who's been through a divorce how it was for them, it's a safe bet they'll answer "it sucked." If divorce is so common, why don't we do a better job of it?

When my parents divorced in the early 1970s, divorce had become common but still wasn't accepted. The scarlet "D" impacted every aspect of their lives, and helpful resources were slim to none.

When I divorced in the early 2000s, things had come a long way. By then, people rarely batted an eye at the scarlet "D," Oprah was nudging us all toward enlightenment, and a fledgling collaborative family law movement was encouraging a less combative legal approach.

Fast forward to 2016: *Conscious Uncoupling* by Katherine Woodward Thomas was made famous by Gwyneth Paltrow's public, pleasant divorce. That book painted a picture of a civil, almost lovely, divorce process. However, if you are going through a divorce right now, that idea may still sound futuristic or even impossible. From where I sit, there's lots of work to do to improve the way we divorce and to reduce the suffering of divorcing and divorced persons like you and me.

You can be a ground-breaker. You can embrace a new version of divorce. And although we all hope that our kids don't go through it, you can show them a better way to handle this tumultuous life event, just in case. If that reward seems too distant, you can also reduce your suffering right now.

Maybe it's hard to imagine a civil, almost lovely, divorce. I get that. I'm no Pollyanna about divorce, with an excessively cheerful disposition and unfailingly optimistic outlook. I don't believe that suffer-free divorce exists or that it ever will. I'm more of a pragmatist. I'm an accountant who is in the divorce business, two things that guarantee me to be a Pollypragmatist instead.

Despite that pragmatism, I know that you can reduce your divorce suffering. Maybe you're saying, "You don't know my situation. My ex slept with my sister, poisoned my cats, ran off with all our money, and always left an empty toilet paper roll." I hear you. But even if your ex is the devil, there are things you can do to make the process easier.

Divorce suffering comes in two forms: suffering caused by your own hurt feelings and twisted thoughts, and suffering caused by untying all the knots in your life, from your living arrangements and shared friendships to your family finances. In this book, my focus is on a combination of helping you untie the knots in your thoughts and feelings, as well as those in your finances. Do these sound like strange bedfellows? Here's the thing: when you're under the influence of twisted thoughts and hurt feelings, it is infinitely harder to untangle your finances. Your thinking and feeling impact the business of your divorce. Healthy thinking is good for business. Twisted thinking is bad for business.

This is why I have structured this book to address your thinking around divorce first, before I get into the financial nitty-gritty of preparing you for your divorce. In part one, I will offer you tools to untwist your thoughts and ease your hurt feelings. As a Pollypragmatist, I have to acknowledge that in this particular scenario you are shooting for "better" not "best." Divorce is a tough time, and twisted thoughts and hurt feelings are part of the package. But if you use these tools to reclaim your power over those thoughts and feelings, you will suffer less. We'll explore how to put all that clear thinking to work with good divorce behavior. I'll also share with you what's important to consider when assembling your divorce A-team so that you are supported with the right people through the business of your divorce.

In part two, we'll dig into the ways in which you'll need to prepare so you can navigate your divorce process with a cool, calm business-oriented mind. If you are tempted to skip over part one and jump to that section, don't. You'll need all the tools I'll share in part one to help you successfully manage the business of your divorce. Then I'll turn you into a master negotiator so you can cross the finish line and begin navigating those early days A.D. (after divorce)!

Before we get started, though, let me share a few things about me.

I am a divorce expert. Lucky me!

Divorce work wasn't my calling of choice as a twelve-year-old. This path didn't come up during any of my high school career counseling sessions. I wanted to be a veterinarian. But here I am.

My training started in childhood with my parents' divorce, then continued with my divorce from my first husband and a close call with my second. But more important than that are my three decades of experience as an accountant and my current focus on exclusively practicing in the area of divorce, helping women navigate the financial implications of complex divorces. Although my divorce work doesn't make me popular at parties, it has become my passion.

To be clear, while I will also share some tips to help you think in a healthier way in order to reduce your suffering during your divorce, I'm not a mental health professional. I'm an accountant who has done a lot of reading and course work, received counseling and coaching, and put the information I've learned into practice. Regardless, a book can never replace professional help. If you need medical or mental health support, please seek advice and guidance from a health professional.

While we're on the subject of things that I'm not, I'm also not a family lawyer. I avoid giving legal advice in this book because I don't want to get sued! But what I can do is show you how to develop a plan for navigating the legal aspects of your divorce.

A big part of my life's purpose is to reduce the suffering of people going through divorce—to reduce *your* suffering. *You* are my "why" for writing this book, and it is my greatest hope that it will help you lay a foundation for a better divorce.

A Note on Language

I dig the written word. I dig words, period. Just ask my family, whom I have occasionally talked to near-death. I believe that words inform our thoughts, which can change our feelings and behavior. And since words are so powerful, I want to address some of the specific language that I've used and the approach that I've taken in this book.

First, throughout this book I refer to your soon-to-be-former mate as your "ex." I understand that you probably aren't officially divorced yet. But since you are getting divorced, ex seems more appropriate than spouse.

Second, I also refer to your former relationship as a "marriage." But that's just to keep things simple. Whether your relationship was a marriage or marriage-like, this book is for you.

Third, I am a woman, a mom and stepmom of daughters, and I work exclusively with women. When writing this book I had women in mind, so my approach, language, and stories demonstrate that gender focus. However, if you'll forgive a wildly self-serving comment, I truly believe that every person going through divorce can benefit from my suggestions and tools.

Finally, I am heterosexual and, so far, all of my clients have been heterosexual. However, as a proud mom of a gay kid, it is deeply important to me that people of all orientations can see themselves in these pages. Who you love or loved doesn't make one whit of difference to your divorce. Unless who you loved turned out to be the devil themself.

These are all my biases laid bare as I have no wish to offend, dismiss, or discount any reader.

ONE

PROTECTING YOUR EMOTIONAL HEALTH

1

Healthy Thinking

Don't believe everything you think.

IF YOU'RE anything like I was during my divorce, depending on the time of day you might be feeling muddled, confused, exhausted, or devastated. Thinking straight might seem like the least of your worries. But I promise that ditching your unhealthy thinking is worth the investment, as it will absolutely help you avoid unnecessary suffering (as if there is *necessary* suffering).

Putting Your Thoughts in Their Place

If your head is spinning with frantic divorce thoughts, it's hard to imagine shifting to healthy thinking. But there are some simple ideas that can help you do exactly that.

Thought Tamer #1: You are not your thoughts

Maybe you've heard this idea before. I first read about it in *The Untethered Soul* by Michael A. Singer. My first reaction—and perhaps yours too—was that this concept is woo-woo. Of course you are your thoughts! However, your thoughts have a conflict of interest. Your thoughts are very attached to themselves, and they want you to be very attached to them too.

In an attempt to make this idea more practical, I'll share with you how I implemented it in my own life. Initially, I got hung up on the definition of "me," along with what to include in that definition. At first, my mind concluded that my thoughts were "me."

Me = Thoughts

Pretty quickly I realized that my body was missing from my equation. So I fixed that, and upgraded my definition.

Me 2.0 = Thoughts + Body

Then, I accepted that "me" should also include my soul or spirit. I mean, a robot has a body, as well as a mind or processing unit. I may have bitten off more than I can chew here, philosophically speaking, but there is something missing from a robot compared to a human. Let's call that something our spirit.

So this was the new "me."

Me 3.0 = Thoughts + Body + Spirit

Now I had a more complete concept of me: thoughts, body, spirit. At this point, I wasn't sure that this concept was going to be of practical use in my life, and my picture was messy (I hate mess). I cleaned it up.

Me 4.0 = Thoughts + Body + Spirit

OK people, now we're talking.

"You aren't your thoughts." This simple idea helped free me. At a minimum, let's call your thoughts one part of you. And, if it fits for you, you could think of the real "you" as the observer—the one hearing your thoughts. I have a mental picture of my observer. She is a tiny creature sitting in the command-central chair in my core. This image gives me perspective, helps me step back from racing thoughts, and creates breathing room. Those racing thoughts aren't "me." They are just things I'm observing, data that I'm taking in. Try it out. Because when you are tormented during divorce, being able to step back from racing thoughts is a valuable tool.

Thought Tamer #2: Your thoughts might not be true

Whoa. Hold your horses. I might have accepted the idea that my thoughts aren't me, but believing that they might be wrong? Slow down, big fella.

Actually, most of us accept the possibility that we might occasionally be wrong. Not often, but occasionally. This is a helpful idea during divorce, when we can get attached to our view of things. Keeping in mind that you might have a few things wrong will be useful. It will help you stay open to new ideas, or to suggestions from your advisers, or to the advice from that friend who tells you that slashing your ex's tires may have unintended consequences, like jail.

If you're interested in a deeper dive into the idea that your thoughts might not be true, I recommend checking out *Loving What Is* by Byron Katie.

Thought Tamer #3:
Your thoughts might not be useful

I have another visual of tiny observer-me for my relationship with my thoughts: she is sitting in the command-central chair, with thoughts flowing by like a river.

Tiny-me gets to choose which thoughts to hang on to. She can let go of the thoughts that make her feel crappy. I don't mean to imply that you should ignore reality, but many of those pain-inducing thoughts aren't reality, they're simply our perceptions or assumptions or stories. When you go through a divorce, your stories become pretty darn negative. That makes it more important to embrace the idea that you get to choose which thoughts to hang on to. You with me?

Thought Tamer #4:
Your thoughts might not be reality

Reality is real. Perception is not. Powerful, huh? Here's what I mean. Reality is the things that happen in our shared experience. Perception is our personal experience of reality. Right now you might be thinking that it's time to step away and get a snack or a cold drink, but stick with me! I'll give you an example.

Here's a typical divorce situation. The reality: Your ex is pushing to take the family home. Your perception: They know I love that house. They don't even want the house. They are just trying to make me suffer. They want me on the streets. I probably will be on the streets. I'll have to move into my parent's basement or couch-surf with friends. No more regular showers for me. And I'll probably lose my job because I'm smelly. In fact, I bet that's exactly what they want. Me—homeless, smelly, and unemployed.

OK, so I'm exaggerating a bit. But not much! One hint that you are dealing with your perception about a situation instead of its reality is how convoluted and twisted an idea has become in your mind. Reality is typically brief (short but maybe not sweet), but often our perceptions are long-winded and twisted up with other thoughts.

When you are evaluating your thoughts, work hard to distinguish between reality and your perceptions. This will help you let go of the crappy thoughts.

Thought Tamer #5: Our experiences are a combination of reality and our perceptions

Our experience isn't reality. Instead, our experience is a combination of reality and our own unique, individual perception, or our "story." You might be saying, "Whatever. My perception *is* reality. I'm really good at perceiving." The

YOUR EXPERIENCE

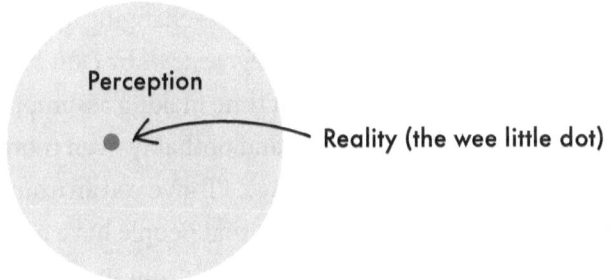

thing is, in our story we are the main character, and in the stories of those around us we are only supporting characters, or even just extras. You know those movies that show a situation from one character's perspective and then run through the same events from a different character's perspective? That's what we are all doing in life. We are all having unique, parallel experiences. It isn't that one person is right and the other is wrong, it's that we are all living in different movies. Clearly, there are some people whose perceptions are closer to yours than others. But nobody, and I mean nobody, sees the world in the exact same way that you see it.

Here is the power of this idea: when you can distinguish between reality and your perceptions, you can change your experience. Boom. Mic drop.

There Is Power in Taming Your Thoughts

There are two cool things that result from using these thought tamers.

Cool Thing #1: You can stop assuming

Don't make assumptions. This is a life-changing idea that I absorbed from reading *The Four Agreements* by Don Miguel Ruiz. We typically spend a lot of time making assumptions about other people's behavior and probably even more so when we are going through divorce. I'll give you an example.

Where I practice, the law says that people have a claim on gifts they've given their partner during the marriage. So, let's say your ex wants to be compensated for half of the massive diamond necklace they gave you when your second child was born after thirty hours of labor and no drugs. Let the assumptions start flowing: They never loved me. They're punishing me because I don't want to be with them anymore. They're going to use the money to buy a necklace for their new love interest.

Now don't get me wrong. I'm *not* saying that they loved you, or that they aren't trying to punish you, or that they won't use the money to buy a necklace for their new love interest. What I *am* saying is that you have no clue about their motivation. Don't waste your time and energy trying to guess what's going on in your ex's head or heart, because there are a million possibilities. The less you can focus on why your ex is behaving a certain way, the better.

Cool Thing #2: You can choose your story

Divorce puts story engines into high gear. You become super attached to your stories and want other people to believe those stories too. Maybe because divorce is a lonely time, you tell yourself that anybody would feel this way if they were in your shoes. But anybody in your shoes would be having their own completely different experience. Who knows how they would feel? If you can accept that there isn't one common, natural reaction to any situation, then you'll be able to examine your chosen story with some objectivity. And if the story is causing you suffering, maybe you can pick a different one.

Have you ever watched *The Matrix* with Keanu Reeves? Minus the leather trench coats, that movie provides an illustration of this ability to choose your own story. If a great big chunk of your experience is simply your perception, your own personal movie, then it makes sense that you can change it, control it, stop bullets in midair. After all, you are the screenwriter and director of your perceptions.

At first you might be so attached to your stories that it's difficult to distinguish between reality and the stuff you make up. But it gets easier with practice. Once you buy into the idea that your experience is your own make-believe, you can choose to make up better stuff.

When I first experimented with this idea, I started small. If a stranger did something that I decided was rude, such as cutting me off in traffic or going through the express line at the grocery store with forty items, I would make up a story that justified their behavior. The guy who cut me off in traffic is racing to the hospital because his wife is in labor. The woman in the express line is distracted because her mom has just been diagnosed with early-onset dementia.

This process eliminated my irritation and helped me distinguish between reality and stories.

It didn't matter if the story I had made up was inaccurate. Maybe the guy who cut me off was rushing to his mistress's house for a quick one while his wife was in labor. Maybe the woman in the express line didn't give a crap about the fifteen-item limit. But it didn't matter, because when I made up those better stories, my life improved. Before I got intentional about making up stuff that made me feel good, my stories were negative. Whatever the reason, our stories usually are pretty negative—until we examine them, challenge them, and choose something better.

If we're already inclined to be negative at the best of times, then getting divorced can make us positively foul. Your ex brings you flowers? They're a scheming jerk who wants to know if you had someone over for dinner. An acquaintance asks how you're doing? She's a prying gossip who can't wait to report on you at her next book club. How cool if you could choose something better. Your ex wants a healthier relationship with you and has extended an olive branch with the flowers. That acquaintance truly cares about how you're doing. You've always liked her and perhaps this is an opportunity to get closer.

It isn't that the positive stories are more accurate than the negative stories. In the end both versions are simply stories, neither true nor false. The positive ones just make you feel better!

Debunking Relationship "Fairy Tales"

Collectively, we've wrapped stories around big relationship events like divorce and marriage. Unfortunately, many of us still buy into these stories, and they're often a cause of much suffering, especially where divorce is concerned. It's worth debunking these "fairy tales" if you want to lessen your suffering.

Fairy Tale #1: I'm marrying my soulmate

I get the appeal of this fairy tale. It sounds pretty magical, and who doesn't want some magic? But let's dissect this tale. It goes like this: There is only one person out there with whom you have a fated soul connection that may or may not be repeating across time and space. You are one another's destiny, and you just need to find each other and live happily ever after.

The tricky part of this story is its false conclusion: if you find your soulmate, then you won't have problems, or at least you won't have big, bad problems that lead to divorce. If you subscribe to the soulmate story, then coping with divorce also involves the perceived loss of your soulmate. Or, it can inspire the development of a new story: I guess I didn't actually marry my soulmate. I got it wrong. I've got to keep looking.

Even allowing for the soulmate possibility, we are still imperfect humans and our soul connections are tainted by imperfection. Even soulmates can have big, bad problems and get divorced. So let's tweak the soulmate story to include the possibility of more than one soulmate. And, while we're at it, let's include the understanding that finding and marrying your soulmate might end with you also divorcing your soulmate.

Fairy Tale #2: Marriage is forever

Even if you don't subscribe to the soulmate theory, on your wedding day you're typically optimistic about your relationship. That optimism often includes the belief or hope that it will last forever. Most wedding vows include some kind of "forever" commitment. Sickness and health, good times and bad and all that jazz. Certainly, this kind of commitment is romantic and, for some, an enduring marriage is a religious expectation. But the story that marriage is supposed to be forever can increase suffering during divorce. Maybe some marriages aren't meant to be forever. And maybe that's perfectly fine.

Fairy Tale #3: If a marriage ends, it was a failure

I don't consider my first marriage a failure, although I heard through the grapevine that my ex described it as such. Maybe he has since reconsidered. Either way, I'm grateful for our fourteen years together. I didn't have kids with my first husband, so it isn't the old "I can't stand that guy but I love my kids, so it wasn't a total waste of time" classic. I truly loved him. He was my high school sweetheart, and we grew up together. He was a kind, loyal, funny companion. To strip away everything wonderful about the years we spent together because one of us didn't die at the end seems like crap to me. Obviously, there was some not-so-good stuff. But it wasn't a failure.

If you hang on to this kind of failure story, then you'll be listening to it run through your mind over and over as you deal with your split. Each decision you have to make, every email you receive from your ex or your lawyer will remind you of your perceived failure and will make your divorce much harder.

Using only one measure of success for marriage—that it only ends when one partner dies—is darn limited. If one or both people are miserable, is the marriage a success? If a marriage is plagued by infidelity, addiction, abuse, or neglect, is it a success? If you enjoyed twenty great years and then decided to part, is the marriage a failure? Let's think more broadly about the definition of a successful marriage.

Fairy Tale #4: Divorce will damage your kids

At the time I was first writing this section, my second husband and I were separated. At year thirteen we had a close call with divorce, and we spent that entire year apart. We are the parents of two kids, so there was a real possibility then that our kids would have divorced parents. I wanted to make sure that everything I wrote for this book came from conviction and not from the burning desire to believe that I wasn't screwing up my kids. So what follows is the result of considerable reflection, personal experience, and observations of countless examples. It is also strictly my opinion.

I used to be so sure. "Don't stay together for the kids." But when I was thinking about my own kids, all that self-assurance vanished. Nothing tested my convictions more than watching my kids grieve when their dad and I separated. Ours was not the story of a chaotic family life that was creating hardship for our kids, so I couldn't hang my hat on the idea that our separation was better for them. The hard truth is that divorce includes sad times for every member of the family. It's heartbreaking to watch your kids suffer, and it's even worse when you believe it's your fault.

But my goal as a parent isn't to ensure that my kids never experience pain. Pain, sadness, and grief are essential parts of being human. I have evolved the most through the painful times in my life. Most of my close friends and family, too, have had hefty servings of pain and suffering. They have turned that pain into wisdom, empathy, tolerance, and acceptance. It's impossible for me to deliberately manufacture hardship for my kids, but when it finds them, I remind myself that it's an important part of their life. I listen and empathize and help when appropriate, but I can't eliminate the hardship.

Divorce will cause pain and suffering for your kids. It will cause pain and suffering for you. But I believe that this hardship may serve to strengthen your kids instead of damaging them. Still, you have to make a conscious effort to help your kids move through the pain without permanent damage. If you ever needed motivation to embrace healthy thinking and good behavior, here it is.

Fairy Tale #5: If I am divorced, I am damaged goods

Many years ago, when my older sister was newly divorced, she dated a guy who had been married three times. I was a know-it-all twenty-something who was still in my first marriage, and I wondered what was wrong with him. Married and divorced three times? He was damaged goods. As it turned out, he was a decent man and I now cringe thinking about my harsh judgment.

I thought this story would be much easier to debunk than the "divorce damages the kids" story. But I struggled with this one. I did a decent job of explaining the end of my first marriage. I convinced myself that it was an anomaly and that while the situation was messed up, I wasn't. I squirmed around this story the first time. But when I was facing potential marriage breakdown number two, things got trickier. For me, healing the pain from this story came in an unlikely form—acceptance. I accepted that I am damaged goods, sort of like the velveteen rabbit in that children's book, except not as sweet. I am battered, ripped, and stained. Maybe you are too. And I mean that in the nicest possible way. You are the people I like best.

IF YOU can embrace the idea that you aren't your thoughts and that your thoughts might not be true or useful, then you are on your way to freeing yourself from unhealthy thinking. You have a vital foundation on which you can move through your divorce with less suffering. But just when you think you've had attained enlightenment, the raging blame giant or shame troll can rob you of your clear mind. The next chapter will arm you for your fight against those monsters.

> **A Quick Summary**
> - Work on healthy thinking *before* digging into the business of your divorce.
> - You are not your thoughts. You are the observer of your thoughts.
> - Your thoughts might not be true or useful.
> - Your perceptions define your experience.
> - Debunk destructive fairy tales around marriage and divorce. You will suffer less.

2

Ditch Blame and Shame

Blame and shame pollute your divorce and your life.

IN MY WORK as a divorce financial adviser, I am often shocked at how poorly people treat the ones they used to love. I should be used to it by now, but it still rattles me. Honestly, I have yet to find anyone who has not succumbed to their darker self at least one or twice as their marriage falls apart, and that includes me. The things I've seen represent a laundry list of bad human behaviors. I've seen lots of infidelity, slander, and gossip. I've watched people spitefully restrict access to kids and pets, flush loads of cash down the toilet in pursuit of revenge, and hold their ex hostage financially by hoarding all the assets. Sadly, I've also seen super scary behavior, like killing pets and stalking.

The business of divorce is a tough business. Maybe you and your ex behaved like adults as your relationship came to a peaceful end and you're thinking about skipping this chapter. But don't. Divorce is a breeding ground for terrible behavior, so it's best to consider how you'll handle wrongdoing.

You might be thinking, "Why bother? I'm getting divorced, after all. I don't have to live with that jerk anymore. I'm free to hold a grudge forever." It's also easy to think that we can put our own bad behavior in a box and shove it into a back corner of our minds.

The thing is, during divorce most people create a long list of stuff for which they blame their ex. And then another long list of stuff about which they feel shame. But if you hang on to all that blame and shame, it will continue to pollute your life, and the toxic vibe will negatively impact your divorce. Blame and shame create suffering during divorce, so let's talk about ditching them both.

The Blame Game

Say that your ex is the world's worst human being and your blame list is long. When I encourage you to ditch the blame, I'm not protecting or defending them. I'm protecting and defending *you*. I'm protecting your mental health, your relationships with others, and your ability to strike a good deal. And I'm defending you from getting emotionally stuck in your divorce for the rest of your life.

Here are some specific reasons to ditch blame.

Reason #1: You'll learn from your divorce

You won't learn anything from your divorce if you are stuck in a blame game. OK, maybe that's a bit extreme. How about: you won't learn *as much* from your divorce if you are stuck in blame. If you blame your ex for the end of your marriage, you may avoid examining your own contribution. And if you don't examine your contribution, you won't see where you screwed up and where you might make a different choice next time. You will carry your unhelpful behaviors into your next relationship.

Instead, learn what to do differently so you don't wake up in fifteen years in the same position with another partner. Learn from my mistake.

I wasn't aware of blaming my first husband for our divorce. The blame was disguised in my thinking as the idea that we weren't a good match. But, frankly, I was blaming him. I didn't work to figure out my contribution to our problems, so I didn't take responsibility or learn from my mistakes. It wasn't until the near end of my second marriage that I saw how I had repeated some of my destructive behavior from my first marriage.

Here's an example: When things started to head south between me and my first husband, I withdrew from him. But I don't do well when I withdraw. I like being super-duper connected to my mate and, when I withdraw, my soul starts to shrivel up. The result? The relationship heads further south.

The same thing happened when my second marriage hit a rough patch. If I had examined my contribution to my first divorce instead of simply blaming my ex, maybe I could have avoided my second close call with divorce. Blaming almost cost me my second marriage.

Take off the blame-goggles and figure out your contribution to the end of your relationship. Because if you don't work through those issues, they will follow you around. Sure, your ex contributed to the problems in your marriage, but their contribution is their problem, and theirs alone to figure out. You'll benefit from staying focused on your own contribution.

Reason #2: You'll take control of your emotional well-being

Getting stuck in blame means handing over control of your emotional well-being to your ex. Blame isn't about judging someone's behavior as crap. Blame is about pointing to that behavior as the reason why you feel like crap. Blame is the link between the bad behavior and the impact of that behavior on you.

This is you when you blame:

This is you when you let go of blame:

Better, right?

Blaming means viewing yourself as a victim and your ex as a villain. But in that simplified view of reality, you are powerless. And that's a vulnerable way to live. We don't control the world around us, but we do choose the way we perceive and relate to the world. You are not a victim of life, but you will be a victim of your own thinking if you choose to regard yourself as powerless.

One of the payoffs you get when you hang on to blame is that people feel bad for you. They may even want to save you. But allowing that to happen is simply another way you hand over the control of your emotional well-being to others. Better to stand on your own two feet. Two healthy feet. Are you with me?

Reason #3: You'll avoid seeking revenge

In my work, I've seen many people who are stuck in blame go on to seek revenge—in fact, I've had a front-row seat to this show. I've seen it enough times that I know how it ends. Spoiler alert: revenge does not alleviate pain. Not one little bit. It's sort of like eating fast food. It seems like a good idea, but afterward you feel like crap. Even worse, revenge also comes at a high price: legal fees, emotional energy, and your time. So let's safely conclude that seeking revenge is an all-around bad idea.

If you need more convincing, here's another angle to consider. Revenge can lead to unintended collateral damage. Your kids, friends, or boss might think you took things too far with that whole tire-slashing business. Still don't believe me? Then believe some ancient wisdom: "Before you embark on a journey of revenge, dig two graves."

Shaking off Blame

Now that you know why blame sucks, the next trick is learning how to shake it. Here are three ideas for doing just that.

BLAME

Blame Shaker #1: Take responsibility for your contribution

Get over the idea that the only thing you did wrong was pick the wrong person to marry. You may say, with great maturity, that you know it takes two to screw up a marriage. But until you get specific about your contribution, a little voice in your head will keep saying, "Sure. But in this case, it was mainly them"—and then the blame will be hard to shake. I don't know you, so there is no way you can take this personally, but it's likely that you contributed more than simply tolerating the bad behavior of your ex. You are human. There must be more to it. Of course, if you were abused in the marriage, this will entirely overshadow your contribution to the dysfunction of that marriage. But I still believe there is value in examining your contribution even if what you discover is that you endured abuse out of fear for your emotional and physical well-being.

Take the time to explore, no matter how painful, how you may have contributed to your marriage woes, and I promise: you'll take a big step toward shaking off the blame, and freeing yourself to move forward.

Blame Shaker #2: Avoid playing the victim

Your ex just maxed out your joint credit card by paying for an extravagant trip to Vegas with the new love interest. If you see yourself as a victim, you might have this reaction: "He makes me furious. He is ruining my finances."

But if you don't play the victim, you might have this reaction instead: "I am furious. I am not going to allow him to ruin my finances. I am canceling the joint credit card."

Letting go of victimhood can be a difficult shift in your perspective. Horrible things happen to people during divorce. And when bad things happen, you deserve great heaps of love and empathy. But you don't need to view yourself as a victim, even if the only power you have in a situation is to determine how you think about it and how to respond. In his book *Man's Search for Meaning*, Viktor Frankl described his experience as a survivor of four concentration camps. He did not view himself as a victim, despite being subjected to indisputable horrors. Instead, he embraced the only freedom he had: the ability to choose his thoughts and perspective.

One key to ditching the victim role is embracing the reality that nobody and nothing *makes* you feel anything. When you drop the victim role, you take control. You control the perceptions that shape your experience. You control your response to your experiences. And that's a heck of a lot safer than handing that control over to your ex.

Blame Shaker #3: Don't take it personally

This might sound ridiculous in light of how personal everything feels when you are getting divorced. But here's what I mean. Let's say your husband just told you he wants a divorce. He has another wife and child in Brazil and has decided to pull up stakes and move to live with them. He tells you that if you had only cooked better food or laughed harder at his jokes or spent less time with your friends, then you wouldn't have forced him to find another wife. That feels pretty darn personal. But seriously? That dude is wrong. His horrible behavior is the result of his crappy choices. His crappy choices are a result of the unique cocktail of who he is, shaken and stirred with his experiences.

Of course, that he has another wife and child also feels pretty darn personal. And of course you have strong personal thoughts and feelings about it. But understanding that it's about him and not you should help you lower your emotional temperature. You will have a better sense of where he ends and where you begin, and you'll be on your way to untangling from him and his behavior. And that will put you on your way to shaking the blame.

Remember, shaking off blame doesn't eliminate the expectation that people should behave well. Your husband should not have another wife and child in Brazil. Shaking blame simply reduces the suffering you experience as a result of that bad behavior.

Blame's Evil Twin, Shame

We all know a lot more about shame, thanks to Brené Brown. Bless her dang heart. Her work has helped me reduce the destructive impact of shame in my life, which has been life-changing.

I was plagued with feelings of shame over my behavior during my divorce. One thing in particular had a strong hold on me. I had been super close to my ex's parents. I loved them and I felt loved by them. I started dating their son when I was sixteen years old, so I had spent loads of time with them as I grew up. I have great memories of eating popcorn, drinking diet pop, and watching TV with my mother-in-law. Family dinners on Sundays were the best, complete with the butteriest garlic bread ever and after-dinner garden tours with my father-in-law, who was a passionate gardener and who sparked that passion in me. When my ex and I initially separated, I maintained a relationship with my in-laws, but I didn't keep that up despite their diligent attempts. Looking back, I don't think I could face their grief or my shame.

If guilt is a feeling of sadness, repentance, or disappointment over something that we've *done*, then shame is a feeling of sadness, repentance, or disappointment over something that we *are*. For me, shame has been my personal cross. I find it tough to ditch even though I know that it's useless. Shame ties up your mind, body, and spirit in miserable knots. Unfortunately, divorce is a breeding ground for guilt and shame. Guilt can be useful if it leads to better future choices. But shame just serves to increase our suffering without much added value in the way of personal transformation.

Twenty years after my divorce, I still feel terrible about distancing myself from my former in-laws. Without a doubt, I would make a different choice today. But here's the thing: I can't undo what I did. Even though distancing myself from them was a crappy move, it doesn't mean that I am crap.

That important distinction can free you from shame. Your actions sucked. But that doesn't mean that you suck. There is a difference between what you do and who you are. So, go ahead and judge the crap out of your actions. Go ahead and vow never to make those mistakes again. But don't conclude that you are a terrible person because of your mistakes.

Here are a few reasons why you should avoid the shame game.

Reason #1: You'll learn from your divorce

Just like blame, shame prevents you from learning from your mistakes. That sounds strange, but shame blots out your ability to focus on what you've done, because you're focused on who you are. Shame, contemplating how worthless you are, leads to... nowhere... except more shame.

If you are wallowing in shame, you are so focused on how bad you are that you often avoid digging in further and examining the bad stuff you've *done*. Clearly, it's not fun to contemplate the bad stuff you've done. But in doing so, at least you get the benefits of learning and transforming. Making a decision that "hey, that was a bad choice and I'm not going to do that again" is much better than continuing down the dead-end road of shame.

Reason #2: You'll avoid getting stuck in the past

The fuel that sustains shame is our past. Assuming that you haven't been living under a rock, you know that "living in the moment" is all the rage. This phrase triggers the grumpy old man in me. I prefer a balance of the past, present, and future. The past represents learning, the present represents experiencing, and the future represents opportunity. That's all good stuff. Of course, there's also bad stuff. The past holds regret, the present holds pain, and the future holds fear. Still, a full life includes living in the past, present, and future. When we get stuck in shame, we get stuck in the past.

Reason #3: You'll avoid paying financial penance

When I decided to end my first marriage, I felt shame. I was breaking the most important promise that I had ever made. My husband was a lovely person, and hurting him felt all kinds of terrible. I wanted to pay penance: self-punishment inflicted as an outward expression of repentance. I thought that might ease the sting of my shame. With that in mind, I walked away from most of our assets.

In this case we were young, so "most of our assets" didn't amount to much and I was able to rebuild. But paying penance with your finances is a risky proposition. What if you can't rebuild? Your shame may pass eventually, but your dark, damp basement suite could be a persistent reality.

In a nutshell, shame leads to penance, and penance, just like revenge, doesn't work. Making yourself suffer because you are ashamed of what you did will not erase the suffering you caused. But paying financial penance can have long-term negative consequences on the quality of your postdivorce life.

Shaking off Shame

SHAME

Now that we've covered the why, let's cover *how* you can shake the shame. Here are five ideas.

Shame Shaker #1: Remember that good people do bad things

You've done bad things and you're feeling like a bad person. You're feeling shame. But ask yourself this question: can good people do bad things?

And, lucky you, I have the answer: of course!

Think of the best person you know. Do you honestly believe that they have never done a bad thing? Of course they have! Everyone has! Hopefully this understanding helps you move past the overwhelming thought that you are crap so you can move on to thinking about all the crappy things you've done. Way better. Or, at least, a bit better and more productive.

Shame Shaker #2: Finish unfinished business

When I was newly separated during marriage almost-breakdown number two, a close friend of mine told me this: "The only way to deal with shit is to go through it. You can't go around it." So uplifting. I made her pay for lunch, but she nailed this idea.

Take the example of my former in-laws. I severed my relationship with them to avoid dealing with their pain. I was trying to go around the shit but it didn't work. Instead, it has stuck with me for coming up on two decades.

Consider your own unfinished business. Maybe you need to listen to your ex explain the pain they experienced when they discovered your infidelity (I'll talk more about the consequences of infidelity later in this chapter). Maybe you need to apologize for leaving town for six months instead of working through the end of your marriage. Whatever it is, get it done. And when you get it done, a path is cleared for you to move forward into acceptance and out of shame. Or at least there is less stuff blocking that path.

Shame Shaker #3: Don't play the hero

It is Christmas 2010. My blended family includes five kids ranging from two to sixteen years old. I am working full-time as a partner in an accounting firm, and my husband is frequently traveling on business. My little ones are at home full-time and my stepkids half-time. I am often asked, "How do you do it all?" To which I reply: "It's no big deal," while swishing my superhero cape.

Christmas preparations begin, and I am decorating, baking, entertaining, shopping, wrapping. I cook Christmas dinner for the family on Christmas Eve. I'm up late putting the finishing touches on Christmas morning—and, when Christmas morning arrives, I'm officially an exhausted nub. Unwrapping begins and is a happy scene of many kids enjoying large stockings full of individually wrapped items. My oldest opens one of those individually wrapped items and hands it to me explaining that she doesn't like it and

I can return it. I lean toward her and quietly explain that she can "fucking pretend you like it for at least a week."

You wouldn't believe how much everyone loved their gifts that year.

Up to that point in my parenting career, none of my kids had heard me swear. In that moment, I saw the underbelly of trying to be a hero. I saw that I had the capacity to become an exhausted and foul-mouthed nub when I pushed it too far. From then on, I began a long rehabilitation. Now we buy Christmas dinner from a local hotel, I shop online, and hubby helps me wrap. He hates it; but he knows the alternative, so he doesn't complain.

In the same way that blame is connected to playing the victim, shame is connected to playing the hero. A hero takes care of everyone. A hero is powerful and amazing and so who doesn't want to be a hero? But playing the hero has a few serious limitations. First, you ignore your own needs. Which can be hard to sustain and can lead to hitting the wall. Discovering you are human after all can be hard to accept. (Take it from a recovering hero: it can definitely be hard to accept.) And second, you view people around you as victims who need saving. That is not the best recipe for equality in your intimate relationships. Being a hero is a lonely existence. Ask Wonder Woman.

Better to voluntarily step off the pedestal than to fall off from exhaustion. Be prepared that it might feel like a loss at first. But let's be honest—you aren't a superhero and pretending to be one is a bit ridiculous. (I mean that in the nicest possible way, since I also spent many years pretending.) Let my Christmas 2010 be a warning to you to get off the hero pedestal.

Shame Shaker #4: Be kind to yourself

When working to ditch shame, show yourself the same kindness that you show others. I'm sure you've bought into the idea that you should be kind to others. I bet you're good at that. But what about when it comes to you? I'm guessing you aren't so kind to yourself. All of us tend to be critical, even downright unkind, when it comes to ourselves. Turn that around and watch how it helps to melt shame.

Shame Shaker #5: Choose to transform

My brother told me how he used to constantly leave the cupboard doors open in the home that he shared with his girlfriend. He said the first time it happened, she asked him to close them. The tenth time, she yelled at him. After the ten-thousandth time, she kicked him out. I'm guessing there was more to it, but it's a great illustration of the destructive impact of repeated offenses. Sure, maybe my brother apologized for each cupboard-door fiasco, maybe he even beat himself up about it. But if instead he had transformed into a cupboard-door-closer, he would have rocked her world, and I might have gotten a niece or nephew out of the deal.

Instead of shackling yourself with shame, choose to transform. Maybe you won't have the opportunity for a redo in your former relationship, but I guarantee you'll get another opportunity to behave poorly or to make a better choice.

The Magic Bullet of Forgiveness

When it comes to ditching blame and shame, there is a magic bullet that's often overlooked. That magic bullet is forgiveness: forgiveness of others and forgiveness of yourself.

For me, forgiveness of others comes relatively easy. I was raised by Christians—much better than wolves—so I had an early introduction to the concept of forgiveness in Sunday school.

Fast-forward to my middle teens when my mom went through some health challenges that involved an extended hospital stay. My stepdad took care of me while my mom was away. As a self-centered teenager, I felt like my mom abandoned me. So, when she came home, I wasn't super welcoming. I don't have a ton of vivid memories about this chapter in my life, but this one is powerful. My mom and I were standing in the kitchen, and she said quietly, "Your dad must have taken good care of you." I realized that I was holding a grudge against my mom. I made the decision to let go of my grudge and forgive her. (From my adult perspective, I realize she didn't need forgiving.) That forgiving translated my Sunday school lessons into a life-altering enlightenment. When I forgive others, I feel better.

Forgiveness isn't about condoning bad behavior. It isn't for the benefit of the wrongdoer. In fact, you can forgive someone and decide that you no longer want to have anything to do with them. Forgiving others is one of the best things you can do for yourself. It frees you from the pain and suffering of the past.

I've witnessed forgiveness for lying and stealing, for slander and gossip, for infidelity, and it has all worked magic in the lives of others. And, without exception, the act of forgiving has reduced suffering.

In the same way that we often find it easier to extend kindness to others than to ourselves, it is often easier to forgive others than to forgive ourselves.

Let's consider a couple of the reasons you might resist forgiving yourself.

Barrier #1: "I don't deserve forgiveness"

Maybe you don't believe you deserve forgiveness. But forgiveness isn't earned. It's simply *given*. Remember, forgiveness isn't about condoning bad behavior. It's simply a choice to move forward, free from the effects of that bad behavior. I'd like to pitch the idea that your life and the lives of everyone around you will be vastly improved if you become a forgiver. I guarantee that it will not lead to an explosion of wrongdoing. It will lead to a reduction in your suffering.

Barrier #2: "I'll repeat my mistakes if I forgive myself"

I used to worry that if I forgave myself for a mistake, I would risk repeating that mistake. But strangely, I've found that the opposite is true. When I got stuck in shame and didn't forgive myself, I worked hard to avoid even thinking about my mistakes, and about the people I'd hurt, like my former mother-in-law. Over the years, I got freaky good at compartmentalizing. I put my mistakes in individual boxes organized neatly on shelves in my mind, but I left them unlabeled so I could avoid any reminders. As a pragmatist, it finally struck me that ignoring my mistakes might not be the best way to avoid repeating them. If you forgive yourself then you won't have to avoid thinking about your mistakes. You can examine them, learn from them, and not repeat them.

Infidelity: The Mother Lode of Blame and Shame

Now that you've got some tools to help you ditch blame and shame, let's talk about one of the toughest and most common situations in which you will need to use those tools: infidelity.

It's a rare couple that gracefully drifts apart without behaving terribly toward one another. And infidelity is often one of those terrible behaviors. Maybe it's sex with or an emotional attachment to someone else, or extreme neglect of the relationship through a focus on work. But let's zero in on the kind of infidelity that creates the most chaos: sex with someone else. Everyone affected by infidelity is emotional about it. Even people who haven't been affected by infidelity are emotional about it. Here is some straight talk for both the cheater and the cheated.

To the cheater: You screwed up big time. And although you may have your reasons, you better not talk about them for a long, long time or perhaps ever. You made a monumentally bad choice when you decided to be unfaithful instead of addressing your issues directly. Don't look for ways to defend yourself instead of owning your mistake. Instead, be genuinely sorry and genuinely apologize, because any possibility of your divorce sucking less depends on it.

To the cheated: I am deeply sorry that you have suffered through your ex's infidelity. It's terrible. But it doesn't mean that your relationship was a lie. It doesn't mean that you were stupid, gullible, or blind because you didn't see it earlier. And it doesn't need to be the defining element of your relationship with your ex as you move through your divorce and beyond.

To both the cheater and the cheated: What follows are a few things you can both do to get through this.

Strategy #1: Get help

You will both benefit from some professional help. Preferably from a counselor experienced in working with people who are dealing with this brand of trouble. If the idea of talking through the issue with a virtual stranger makes you feel uncomfortable, I recommend GoAskSuzie.com for a mountain of helpful resources and strategies for both the cheater and the cheated.

Strategy #2: Choose your supporters wisely

You'll need support from friends and family to get through this tough time. But choose those people wisely. If you are the cheated, don't surround yourself with people who will simply vilify your ex and add fuel to the existing rage-fire that is likely burning inside you. If you are the cheater, don't surround yourself with people who will simply vilify your ex and add ammunition to your aggressive defense for your screw-up.

Strategy #3: Be slow to act

When in doubt, do nothing! If you are the cheated, calling your newly minted ex's boss with all the gory details might feel darn satisfying—until your ex can't pay the bills because they are unemployed. If you are the cheater, going on a Vegas getaway with your love interest might feel darn satisfying—until everyone in your family and community thinks you are a complete douchebag. Better to do nothing. And wait for your sanity to return.

Strategy #4: Do not involve your kids

Your kids can barely stand to think about their parents having sex with each other, let alone that one of you had sex with someone else. If you are the cheated, it might be tempting to tell your kids. Maybe they will take your side. But that means they might view one of their parents as a villain, and nobody wants to have an evil parent. Just ask Luke Skywalker.

If you are the cheater and your ex has told your kids about it, the temptation to defend yourself will likely be strong. Maybe you'll want to explain all the terrible things your ex did that pushed you to cheat. But no kid wants to take sides against a parent. If your ex has told your kids about your infidelity, don't indulge in the temptation to retaliate. Apologize and show them you are not a villain.

SO, YOU'VE chosen healthy thinking and you've worked to ditch blame and shame to reduce your suffering. Now your mind is on your side! Feels good, doesn't it? Time to put all this healthiness to work out in the real world. Next, let's talk about good divorce behavior and how that good behavior will get you good results.

A Quick Summary

- Ditching blame helps you learn from your mistakes and take control of your emotional well-being.

- Ditching shame helps you avoid getting stuck in the past and paying financial penance.

- Forgiveness is the magic bullet that dispels both blame and shame.

- If you are coping with infidelity, get help.

3

Good Behavior Gets Good Results

When you behave well, you suffer less.

AS I'VE TOLD you, I've seen my share of bad behavior while working in the divorce business, and remember, I've behaved badly myself. I ghosted my in-laws. But more than that, many of my friendships suffered as I turtled, socially speaking, during my divorce. When I emerged from my divorce haze, I found that I had lost connection with many friends who would have eased the pain of my divorce and improved my life after that divorce.

Speaking from experience, I encourage you to be on your best behavior during your divorce. Or, given that you will no doubt face experiences that test your resolve, at least do your best to behave.

The High Road Is Worth It

Maybe you're thinking: "Why? My ex isn't behaving well. Besides, I feel like crap and I have no energy to worry about my behavior." I get it. But good behavior will get you good results. Here's what you can expect if you put in the effort.

Result #1: You'll feel better

Behavior is one part of a three-part cycle that can either be vicious or positive. That is the cycle of behavior, thoughts, and feelings. If you have embraced the ideas from chapters 1 and 2, you have already begun creating a positive spin with healthy thinking and the lighter feelings that come with ditching blame and shame. You can reinforce this positive momentum with your good behavior. It makes sense that healthy thinking leads to feeling better, which leads to good behavior. But I have also observed that, during divorce, good behavior leads to healthier thinking, which leads to feeling better. I have observed that when people behave well during their divorce, they remain calmer. Regardless of the divorce storm swirling around them, their own good behavior seems to keep them in the eye of that storm. Maybe it's a protective force field?

I strongly encourage you to resist destructive behavior. Behavior like standing in the driveway cursing your ex's name while they speed off in their new hot rod after dropping the kids off late, then killing a bottle of wine and passing out on your neighbor's lawn, then finally resisting arrest because your neighbors called the cops to complain about the noise and the drunk on their lawn.

Instead, use the power of the behave-think-feel cycle to your advantage. Thank your ex for bringing the kids home safe and sound, and politely ask them to shoot you a text next time they're going to be late. That may lead to thinking about how they are a reliable co-parent, which might lead to you feeling more relaxed and optimistic, which is way better than feeling hungover and incarcerated.

Good behavior leads to good feeling.

Result #2: You'll preserve your relationships

Divorce means losing of one of your primary relationships. Even if it sucked near the end, it probably filled a lot of space in your life. During your divorce and beyond, the other relationships in your life become more important for your health and happiness. You don't want to compound the loss of your spouse with the loss of, or damage to, your relationships with your kids, extended family, friends and colleagues, or community. Instead, you want to preserve and protect those relationships. The way you behave during your divorce will affect those relationships. People are watching, especially those closest to you.

Result #3: You might build a new relationship with your ex

I saved this result for last because it is likely that you don't want anything to do with your ex right now. That's a common reaction. But even if you can't imagine having a postdivorce relationship with your ex at the moment, that might change. Like, for instance, when you are celebrating your grandson's first birthday. You will feel comfortable, and your daughter will be thrilled to have both of her parents in attendance at the same time, as opposed to in shifts.

You want to hear something odd? You might even have a better relationship with your ex after your divorce. Your good divorce behavior preserves your opportunity to build a positive postdivorce relationship with your ex.

The Be-Do-Have Model

Let's say you like the sound of those good results. But how do you manage to behave well during divorce? Divorce doesn't exactly bring out the best in any of us. Here's an idea: try the "Be-Do-Have" model, which was first illustrated by Stephen Covey in his book *The 7 Habits of Highly Effective People*.

Put simply, and with apologies for the terrible grammar, when you are good, you behave good, and you get good results. Let me illustrate:

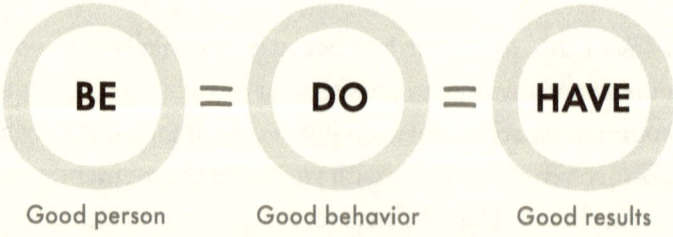

BE = DO = HAVE

Good person   Good behavior   Good results

In my twenties and thirties, my approach to getting good results was the reverse of that model. Here's what it looked like for me then:

HAVE = **DO** = **BE**

Results   Stuff to achieve results   Who cares?

I knocked off a lot of goals. My "Have-Do-Be" approach worked—until it didn't.

My kids were little. The kind of little where I was still involved in the details, like brushing their teeth. In the evenings I was focused on outcomes: get the kids fed and in bed with clean teeth. Mission accomplished. But there was something wrong.

During my mom self-assessment, I identified opportunities for growth. I was impatient, demanding, and inaccessible with my little ones. That sounds harsh and I want you to like me so let's just say that I wanted to be more patient, less demanding, and more accessible. My focus on results was having unintended consequences. My *Have* was getting in the way of my *Be*.

I made a shift. I put my *Be* (patient, accessible mom) ahead of my *Have* (kids fed and in bed with clean teeth). From the outside looking in, our evenings appeared similar. The kids were still fed and in bed with clean teeth. But I was different. I was more relaxed and flexible, although flexibility is still showing up on my self-assessment as an opportunity for growth many years later, so I'll leave it at "more flexible" as opposed to actually flexible. I was happier. The little ones were happier. Although they were pre-memory so they'll have to take my word for it.

I am not telling you who your *Be* should be. I'm suggesting that you should decide who you want to be and then let that choice guide your behavior.

Pitfalls and Potholes

Now that you're buying into why you might want to behave well during your divorce, and you have a general intention about who you want to be to drive that good behavior, it's worthwhile to review some common behavioral pitfalls. Forewarned is forearmed and all that.

Behavioral Pitfall #1: Abusing technology

Back in my day, if you wanted to write to someone, you used snail mail. You had to track down paper and a pen, write a few versions (since it wasn't easy to correct spelling mistakes), find a stamp and envelope, and go to the mailbox to send it. That slow process created space for sanity to prevail, for the sober second thought, because you can't drive to the mailbox when you are knee deep in a bottle of wine. Today if you want to write to someone, you can text or email in the time it takes you to pick up your phone. Sanity doesn't stand a chance.

Texting is tempting. It's immediate gratification. But if you resist the temptation to use it as a platform to work through the pain and suffering of your divorce, that will give your sanity a fighting chance. That's why you probably want to impose some communication restrictions until you've recalibrated your boundaries with your ex. Like, when your blood doesn't boil every time you hear their name.

To avoid saying something you might regret, don't text your ex. Ever. Don't initiate texts. Don't respond to texts. OK, maybe that's unrealistic. Text in emergencies—and I mean real emergencies, involving hospital visits, death, or dismemberment. Restrict yourself to specific, easy topics. Set a five-word limit on your texts, such as "I'll be there in ten minutes." Wait. That's six words. "Be there in ten minutes."

And then there's the social media post from hell. We've all seen and cringed at those posts where people are trash-talking someone. We cringe for both the poster and subject of the post. Way back before the internet, if you wanted to trash-talk someone to your entire community it took creativity, work, commitment. Door knocking, flyers, loudspeakers. But now if you want to trash-talk someone to your family, friends, community, and high school grad class, you just craft a quick post, maybe add some photos or videos to spice it up, no commitment involved. Easy-peasy.

Clearly, if you broadcast gory details about your divorce, it will hurt your relationship with your ex. But that action can also have unforeseen and unintended consequences. Maybe your mutual friends will extend fewer dinner invitations. Maybe your business will suffer when customers become uncomfortable with your decision to trash-talk. Maybe your kids or your kids' friends will see the gore. Maybe your ex's business will suffer when their customers judge them based on your trash-talking—and you will also suffer from those financial consequences. Let's agree, no virtual trash-talking.

Back in my day, we had more privacy. Now, in order to function in the world, we need to share personal information online, and so we've become comfortable with broadcasting our lives, particularly when we're excited or proud, or when we've lost ten pounds, or we've run a marathon, or taken an amazing trip, or have a hot new partner. Hey, I'm glad you're happy, but don't broadcast things, at least not right now. Instead, celebrate quietly. Show your friends that photo of your new love when you're out for coffee. But don't post it online with #Ifinallyknowwhatloveis or #checkoutthoseabs or #loveofmylife. 'Cause that's just gonna sting.

Also, back in my day (am I dating myself?), you had to camp out in front of someone's house if you wanted to know what they were up to. Now, it's pretty easy to be an armchair detective. It can be hard to look away but, please, look away. Because, in this case, ignorance is bliss. Or, at least, ignorance is less terrible. Do not cyber-stalk your ex. Do not look at the posts of their hot new love with

#truelove or #greatcook or #brilliantandbeautiful. 'Cause that's just gonna sting.

These are the four good online behaviors I recommend you maintain during your divorce:

1. Guard your privacy.
2. Guard your ex's privacy, because their business is your business during divorce.
3. Don't cyber-stalk your ex.
4. Limit your online presence and screen time. Period. Consider a yoga retreat in the middle of nowhere with no Wi-Fi.

Behavioral Pitfall #2: Gossiping

After my second husband and I had reconciled, we were at a swanky function sharing a dinner table with some couples we knew and some we didn't. When the gossip began about the latest couple facing marriage breakdown in our community, I lost it. I hate gossip, gossiping, or being the subject of gossip. When I indulge in it or hear other people indulging in it, I feel the need to shower.

I knew that my husband and I would have been the topic of conversation the year before and another couple sitting at the table who had also weathered a rough patch would have been the topic the year before that. I suggested that we all find a better way to entertain ourselves than gossiping about the pain and suffering of our friends. I might have dropped the F-bomb before storming off to the bathroom to regroup. When I came back to the table, the gossip-starter apologized, and we all shared a figurative group hug while committing to avoid gossip for the duration of the evening. Despite my complete lack of diplomacy, it ended well.

All that preaching aside, I am not immune to indulging in gossip. When I started my concerted effort to eliminate it from my life, again helped along by *The Four Agreements*, I explored what motivates gossip. The answer that resonated with me most is that we are trying to bond by sharing the latest juicy tidbit.

Divorce is a breeding ground for gossip. Assuming you aren't a saint, you've probably indulged in some gossiping about your ex. Divorce is a lonely time. We tell our horror stories about our ex to our friends, family, or the grocery clerk in the hope that they'll commiserate with us and we'll feel less lonely. Since we're human, gossiping is to be expected. But only in moderation!

Gossiping is a shabby way to bond with others, and it can make your friends, family, and the grocery clerk feel super uncomfortable. Not what you want if you are trying to preserve relationships. Besides, unless you are a saint, your ex could probably say a thing or two about you. So, bottom line: when you're tempted to gossip, look for other things to talk about that don't make you feel the need to shower.

Behavioral Pitfall #3: Ranting

Getting divorced requires recalibrating your boundaries with your ex. Marriage is an intimate relationship. Sometimes in intimate relationships, we have to work through challenging issues, and sometimes that includes some ranting. But when we are getting divorced we shouldn't rant at our ex, because we are no longer in an intimate relationship. Unfortunately, it can take some time for that reality to sink in. And while it's sinking in, we might be tempted to rant.

When my kids were in their early teens, they occasionally lived up to all those spooky teenager stories. When that would happen during one of our many drives to kid-related activities, I discovered a way to stay relaxed and calm, or at least less irritated. I imagined that I was just delivering a package, a mean package, and I was not going to let a package get to me. That would be weird. Give this a shot. If you feel the desire to rant at your ex, imagine they're a toaster or a plant. You wouldn't let a toaster get to you, right? That would be weird.

Try to keep your communication with your ex short and sweet. Or at least short. Try to keep it professional and polite. I highly recommend checking out Bill Eddy's book *BIFF* (which stands for Brief, Informative, Friendly, Firm) for some practical guidance on managing divorce communication.

Finally, try not to sweat the small stuff. In one of my all-time favorite movies, *Point of No Return* (the American remake of *La Femme Nikita*), Bridget Fonda's character is a former drug addict who is being trained as an assassin. Her training includes etiquette and elocution, because assassins need to be polite. When one of her co-workers is brutally murdered, and she might be next if she loses her cool, she grits her teeth, smiles, and says, "I never did mind about the little things."

When you are dealing with your ex, be like Bridget and never mind about the little things.

Behavioral Pitfall #4: Screwing up at parenting

Going through a divorce is lonely, so it's natural that you'll lean on the people close to you. Just don't lean on your kids, even if they're adults. Turning your kids into your caregivers or confidants will make the situation worse for them. It's your job as a parent to love and support your kids. Do your best to give them a sense of safety and security.

These are the four golden rules for behaving well with your kids:

1 Don't talk shit about your ex to your kids. Ever.

2 Don't fight in front of your kids. They are already freaked out, and fighting in front of them won't help.

3 Keep them informed about the impacts the divorce will have on their lives. Uncertainty sucks.

4 Apologize when you break rules 1 to 3.

Take some time to examine your behavior toward your ex through your kids' eyes. Consider how your decisions will affect them. Is it worth driving a super hard financial bargain with your ex if it means all four of your kids will be sharing a room at their place? Is it worth getting a court order to sell the boat if it means the kids won't be boating next summer? Your kids are the most likely to experience the collateral damage from your divorce process. Do what you can to deflect the shrapnel from the blast.

When my husband and I made the decision to separate, we were on our Christmas family holiday in Hawaii. We decided to tell the kids right away so they would have time to process the idea with us and not have the pressure of getting up and going to school the next morning. In hindsight it was not the ideal time. Our oldest complained that our timing sucked. I apologized for that lack of judgment.

We were open with the kids about how our separation would affect them. In the first week, my youngest laid out a few expectations, to which I agreed. One of those expectations included that their dad and I would always live together or immediately adjacent to one another. At the time, we were living in a large house with a basement suite and my husband was simply moving downstairs. But, a few months later, the kids and I moved into a new house, and my husband rented a condo ten minutes away. I had failed to live up to my commitment. My littlest grieved. And again, I apologized.

You don't need to be perfect. You can't be perfect. And you can't protect your kids from pain. But consciously and consistently do your best and apologize when your best sucks.

Behavioral Pitfall #5: Assuming your relationships will stay the same

When you get divorced you lose your key intimate relationship, and you also run the risk of losing other important relationships. Tread carefully to preserve the relationships that you feel are worth preserving. But be prepared for a major re-jigging of those relationships for which you being a "married person" was an important element.

Getting divorced means the part of your identity that was attached to your role as married person is lost. This impacts you and those around you to varying degrees, depending on how much you and those around you valued that married person part of you.

When my husband and I were separated, some people weren't bothered that I had transitioned from "married lady" to "single lady." In my work relationships, nothing changed. My clients and colleagues don't work with me because I'm married or single. My book club carried on without a hiccup. Even though most of the members are married, our connection with one another has little to do with our marital status.

But some people did give a crap about my transition, like those "couples-friends," the magical couples whom you both like and they both like you. That you are in a couple is what creates the magic. Understandably, the couples-friends were pretty darn attached to the part of me that was "married lady." As were my ex's "people," the people who were in my life because they are in his life: his family, his high school friends, his hockey teammates. Those people were attached to the part of me that was "married-to-*him* lady."

Still, I'm here to say that you can preserve your solid, important relationships. While I was separated, a couple invited me to a Coldplay concert. They made my third-wheel-ness feel completely normal. That evening was such a gift. Yes, it was an amazing concert, but it felt even more amazing to feel accepted as a "single lady."

It will take some time for people to figure out how to relate to the new single you. Don't judge them too harshly if it takes them a minute to wrap their head around it. Don't judge them too harshly if they pull back from you. The good ones will come around.

Consider taking a break from the people who may be struggling with your transition. Wondering what to do about that regular tennis game with your soon-to-be-ex-sister-in-law? You can always fake tennis elbow. Consider shrinking your circle by pulling back into your core relationships, the people with whom you can be an occasional idiot and they will love you, forgive you, and move on.

And beware the voyeurs. Unfortunately, divorce can function like a car crash in your extended network. People have the yucky tendency to slow down and stare. Maybe because they are worried it might happen to them. Or maybe they are bored. Or maybe they are just jerks. Whatever the reason, steer clear.

One of the silver linings of the divorce-cloud is that you'll discover you have some amazing people in your life. Maybe people you underappreciated or relationships you underestimated. Stick with those people during your divorce. Heck, stick with those people for life.

Don't Knock It Till You Try It

Now that you've shifted your thinking around your divorce, ditched your blame and shame, and are on your best behavior, it's time to think about... reconciliation. "What? Reconciliation? I thought you were going to talk about how to get divorced so it doesn't suck!" Well, I am, but first I want you to think about whether a divorce is really what you want.

If you can't imagine reconciliation—either because you don't want it, or you imagine that your ex doesn't want it, or both—I want you to take a minute to think again. If you are imagining that the path to rebuilding your marriage will be painful and challenging and that it might not work, you're absolutely right. But divorce will also be painful and challenging.

If you don't think your ex would consider reconciliation, take some time to revisit that belief as well. You might be surprised to discover that the door you had imagined was nailed shut, welded closed, vanished into another dimension is actually still there and might just open with a knock.

My husband and I had been separated for almost a year when we were scheduled to attend a swanky family function. We had been working hard to mitigate the impact of our marriage breakdown on our kids and implement a civilized version of divorce. At the same time, we were dealing with the heartache of losing each other and the life we had built together. When the day of said function arrived, my husband decided that he didn't want to attend. He couldn't deal with a family tradition when we were no longer a family. In that moment, I felt the loss I had been working hard to deny. Despite our best efforts, we would no longer be a family. Or at least not the sort of family I had in mind. But that day, after years of difficulty, counseling, and separation, we decided to give our marriage another shot. We attended the swanky family function. And although we didn't instantly regain our status as family, it was the first step on our path to reconciliation.

Look, I know how it feels to be on the verge of divorce. You've made such a huge mess of your relationship that you can't imagine staying together. How could you forgive them? How could they forgive you? How could you ever like each other again, let alone love each other? When my second husband and I hit our rough patch, which is like calling a tornado a bit of bad weather, I read somewhere that relationships can be even better after rough patches.

Back then I thought to myself, "Well, you've never seen a rough patch like this one!" But I was wrong. Relationships *can* be even better after rough patches. Here are my theories about why that is.

Rough Patch Benefit #1: Gratitude

Making it through the near-death of your relationship makes you grateful for all the good stuff. When my husband and I were tucking our kids into bed at night, or now when they tuck us into bed, when we share a laugh remembering a distant memory, or when my stepdaughter comes for family dinner on Sunday and it feels easy, I am filled with gratitude. Because these are times that I know would have been forever lost or dramatically altered with the end of my second marriage. And my gratitude keeps me focused on the good stuff we have together instead of the not-so-good stuff. And now I'm imagining my husband reading this and saying, "What's not good?" So I assure him, it's a short list.

Rough Patch Benefit #2: Honesty, the painful kind

In the year before our separation, my husband and I went to weekly marriage counseling sessions. These were no slack-ass counseling sessions. These were the gory kind. I vividly remember the cold sweats I experienced on the way to counseling when I contemplated my intention to be crap-my-pants honest. And I know for sure that if I had chickened out and avoided the scary truth-telling, I would be a two-time divorcee. Fighting to stay married the second time around was harder than my divorce. But it was the kind of hard that you look back on and say: that was terrifying, but totally worth it. I can't say that about my divorce. I look back on my divorce with sadness for all the hurt that affected him, me, and our families.

When you have given up on a future with a partner, you are both free to tell the truth. You have nothing to lose, since you've already accepted that your relationship is probably lost. Honesty creates an opportunity to get to know one another better, to clear away the old hurts and emotional clutter, and to rebuild your relationship and your life together from a clean slate (or clean-ish, since it's almost impossible to scrub away absolutely all of the shit you have created in the process of coming within an inch of divorce).

Rough Patch Benefit #3: Embracing "you do you"

When you're on the brink of divorce, there is an opportunity to reimagine your marriage. Since the old one is basically dead, this offers you a chance to get creative about your possible future.

I find it sort of odd that the standard vision of marriage is so, well, standard. Like we're all supposed to create the same type of relationship: marry relatively young, accumulate wealth and have kids, live together, travel together, and socialize together until you're a couple of oldies who dress the same, talk the same, and think the same. Just describing it makes the rebel in me break out in a rash. We need to embrace "you do you" a bit more to create marriages that are more durable, more enriching. The only people who need to weigh in on what your brand of marriage should look like are you and your maybe-soon-to-be ex.

We're all different and our needs are all different. Maybe our marriages should reflect that diversity. Would you prefer to live apart some or all of the time? Would you prefer separate holidays? Or to run in separate social circles? Or to watch different Netflix shows? Maybe you want to quit your job, sell the house, and buy an RV and you assumed that your soon-to-be ex wouldn't be into that. But maybe they would surprise you. Maybe they would be into that.

A Final Thought on Reconciliation

Whatever the reason, I am living proof that marriage can be better after a rough patch.

When I was almost one year into my separation from my husband, a friend told me that he had never met anyone who regretted staying together. The pragmatist in me countered with the thought that the people who did regret staying together probably don't talk about it or just divorced later, but I got the point. Do everything in your power to make your marriage work, whether that's counseling, time apart, or yelling and screaming.

This is not to say that divorce is wrong or right. It isn't a moral question. Or at least I don't think it is. But divorce is bloody hard. The stress of navigating a mountain of change. The impact of cutting your financial resources in half. The fracturing of relationships and life rhythms. Maybe all that is scary or intimidating or depressing, but I believe it's best that you're prepared. It's best that you pursue other options if they're available.

Younger-me thought getting divorced was easier than working on a broken marriage. Older-me, with the benefit of my own experience and observing the experiences of others, knows that both options are bloody challenging. You might choose divorce, or it might be forced on you. Either way, know that it's a hard path. Do everything you can to avoid it. Then you'll know that you did your best, and you can move through your divorce with the comfort of that knowledge.

Enough said. If you believe divorce is the right step for you, or if your partner is not open to reconciliation, then the next part of this book will guide you through the nitty-gritty of preparing to get your divorce deal done.

A Quick Summary

- Be on your best behavior during your divorce.

- Use the Be-Do-Have model from page 58 to get good results.

- Avoid common behavioral pitfalls, such as abusing technology, gossiping, or ranting at your ex.

- Take the time to consider reconciliation. Your relationship may just be better after your close call with divorce.

4

Your Divorce A-Team

Divorce is a team effort.

YOU ARE GOING to need professional help. As a divorce professional I am clearly biased, but I'm still right. Divorce isn't a do-it-yourself project.

Defining Your Marriage

Before we start talking about what and who you'll need to get divorced, let's have a look at your marriage—because the nature of the challenges in your divorce will be influenced by your particular style of marriage. In my work, I see three typical marriage styles.

Marriage Style #1: The connected couple

This is the couple who work together, wash dishes together, have common friends, and play golf together every Sunday.

If you were in a connected marriage, you will be carving out a new life, independent from your ex in every area. You will be managing an absolute mountain of change and

untying some tight knots. However, since you and your ex collaborated in all things, you maintained an involvement in all aspects of life, from finances to yard maintenance, and your resulting capability in all areas will be useful as you manage the business of your divorce. That said, you will need the support of an advisory team. There is only so much change that we humans can comfortably handle without support.

Marriage Style #2: The independent couple

This is the couple who have separate careers, divide household responsibilities, have different friendship circles, and play golf with other people every Sunday.

If you were an independent couple, you will likely suffer through less change to your lifestyle than a connected couple. However, since you and your ex employed a "divide and conquer" strategy, you'll need help resuming

responsibility for the stuff that your ex handled. Perhaps your ex worked outside of the home and managed the finances while you took care of kids and the household. During your divorce, you'll be on a learning curve if you've become rusty in managing some areas of life. Surround yourself with advisers who can help you with that learning.

Marriage Style #3: The imbalanced couple

In this style of marriage, one person conducts a huge part of their life outside the marriage and one person lives primarily in the marriage.

If you have been in an imbalanced couple and you were the integrated spouse (the small circle within the larger circle), you will need to develop your independence in many areas. You'll require both technical help and help from confidence builders, such as a counselor and empowering friends and family members.

If you were the independent spouse (that big circle), you will likely be able to manage with some help instead of tons of help.

The Lawyer, the Accountant, and the Counselor

Once you have identified the key challenges that you will likely face in the dissolution of your marriage, invest some time and effort into planning how you'll mitigate those challenges. Here is when your divorce team will make all the difference. Don't skimp on getting help.

When I name the lawyer, the accountant, and the counselor, it isn't the start to a bad joke—these are the three legs of your divorce team stool. You are sitting on the stool. You want to make sure it's got all three legs so you don't crash to the floor.

Divorce is a technical process, so you will need the help of technical experts to manage that process. Hence

the lawyer and accountant. But all the technical support in the world won't mean squat if you can't think straight or get out of bed. Hence the counselor. Well, I say counselor, but it could be a counselor or therapist or coach or shaman—whatever works for you.

Maybe you're just fine. Maybe you're thinking clearly and feeling happy and energized. If so, you should write a book because we all need to know your secret. But assuming that you are like most people going through a divorce, it's a safe bet that you could use some personal help.

It is reasonable to expect that your lawyer will know something about the numbers, and your accountant will know something about family law, and that both of them will try to help you think straight. It is unreasonable to expect that your lawyer will also be a financial expert, or that your accountant will also understand everything about family law, or that either of them will be your counselor. So, in an ideal world, a world in which everyone does everything I say, you will hire a lawyer, an accountant, and a counselor. Let's look a little further into what you need to consider before you make your decision.

A-Team Question #1: Do you need a lawyer?

Family law establishes the rules regarding your split, your rights, and your responsibilities. That means you need to be informed about the law or you'll be flying blind through a process that can have serious implications in your life.

When my first husband and I divorced, we chose the do-it-yourself approach. We directly negotiated our deal, had a family lawyer draft the agreement, and ignored her pleas that we get independent advice. And it turned out fine. That said, we were pretty young and didn't have much money, so our divorce wasn't financially complicated.

When my second husband and I separated, we directly negotiated our deal, had a family lawyer draft the agreement, and ignored her pleas that we get independent advice. And it turned out fine. That said, my almost-ex is a lawyer and I'm a divorce accountant and our personal power is evenly matched.

Looking back, I know it was a risk to go through two do-it-yourself divorce negotiations. In your case, do as I say and not as I do—because you should hire a lawyer. Why? Hiring a lawyer is the best way to get informed about the law. And it's my firm belief that you should be fully informed before you make one of the most important deals of your life.

Maybe you are resisting the idea because lawyers are expensive. I get that. But I encourage you to view it more as a question of value than of cost. If you choose the do-it-yourself route to save on legal fees but fail to make a support claim because you weren't aware of your entitlement, that's not good.

Maybe you are resisting the idea because lawyers turn everything into a battle. I get that too. That's a common misconception. Later, I'll talk about ways to avoid turning your divorce into a battleground. For now, just understand that you can hire a lawyer and maintain a civil divorce.

Here are a few questions to ask yourself when you're wrestling with the question of "lawyer or no lawyer."

1. Do I understand family law or feel comfortable developing that knowledge?
2. Is my divorce super-duper simple? (For example, have you been married for ten minutes and have no shared assets?)
3. Do I feel comfortable dealing directly with my ex?
4. Do I feel lucky? (Just kidding. I'm sorry. I know this isn't a laughing matter.)

If you answered "no" to any of these questions—including the last one—please hire a lawyer.

A-Team Question #2: Do you need an accountant?

Obviously I'm not objective on this topic. As an accountant who practices entirely in the area of divorce, I definitely think you should hire an accountant. Here's my sales pitch.

A big part of divorce is financial in nature and while lawyers are experts in the law, they aren't typically experts in financial matters. So unless *you* are an expert in financial matters, you'll probably need some help. And even if you have that expertise, it's unlikely that you're an expert in divorce financial matters. (If you are, let's hang out and talk shop.)

A divorce accountant digests, analyzes, summarizes, and explains the mountains of financial information that often accompanies the business of divorce. They advise you on the many financial decisions you need to make. They also help you develop your financial plans for during and after divorce.

Here are a few questions to ask yourself when you are wrestling with the question of "accountant or no accountant."

1. Am I a numbers person?
2. Do I understand divorce financial matters?
3. Are the financial aspects of my divorce super-duper simple? (Again, like you've been married for ten minutes and have no shared assets.)

If you answered "no" to any of those questions, please hire an accountant.

A-Team Question #3: Do you need a counselor?

Love, you are going to need help to get through this because divorce comes with lots of mental and emotional challenges. Maybe you've worked with a counselor before. High five. Get them on speed dial. You get to skip ahead to the next section.

For the rest of you, maybe you've never sought out this type of help. Maybe counseling sounds freaky. That was me until about fifteen years ago, and then I had an epiphany. I was watching the movie *Always* with Richard Dreyfuss. It's a corny film about a guy who dies and becomes the guardian angel to his girlfriend's new boyfriend (yes, I know, totally believable). Dreyfuss's character realizes that he had been a crap boyfriend and says something along the lines of, "The pain you feel in death is the love you don't express in life."

Now I don't buy into the idea that some of us reincarnate into guardian angels tormented by earthly regrets, but I did get the point. Translation: "Love your people, because when you're dead it will be too late." It hit me that I wasn't expressing my love for one of my stepdaughters. I mean, I loved her like crazy. But I wasn't showing it because I was scared she wouldn't love me back. I cried for the time I had wasted holding myself back. That epiphany got me thinking that I could use some help with uncovering other areas in my life that might benefit from a bit of fixing. I needed another set of eyes.

For the last fifteen years I have worked with a counselor or a coach. They've helped make my bad times bearable and my good times better. I was working with a coach when my second husband and I were weathering our rough patch. Without her, I'm not sure that our marriage would have survived.

Hire a counselor. You'll suffer less.

A-Team Question #4: What about your friends?

Of course you'll need the help and support of your friends. Friends are wonderful. But please, don't turn to your friends for legal advice, financial advice, or counseling. If divorce professionals had a dollar for every time a client was derailed by irrelevant, inaccurate, or misguided advice from a friend, we could retire in luxury. The business of divorce is complex. Every divorce is unique. Take advice from your experts. Take love and support from your friends.

Can I Do-Some-of-It-Myself?

Even if I've convinced you that divorce is not a do-it-yourself project, you might be wondering whether you can do-some-of-it-yourself. Heck, you are the person getting divorced. You are a capable person with a good head on your shoulders. Surely you can handle some of this on your own?

Agreed. You can handle some stuff on your own. In fact, you'll need to because even when you hire professionals, you are the one getting divorced. Even if you delegate, you remain the final decision-maker.

There can be benefits to handling some stuff on your own. It's free, for one thing. And since you are the decision-maker, it's efficient. Still, I get a little nervous when I think about you doing-some-of-it-yourself, so I'm going to calm my nerves by giving you some advice.

Before you go it alone and handle a divorce issue yourself, consider the following questions.

DIY Consideration #1: What is the nature of your relationship with your ex?

If your relationship with your ex includes a reasonable balance of power, and if it's civil, then you're off to a good start. Feel free to move on to the next questions to determine whether you can handle certain stuff on your own. However, if you feel intimidated by your ex, or if they are behaving erratically, don't bother reading the rest of the questions because you will need the support of your team to handle all the stuff.

DIY Consideration #2: Do you understand your rights and responsibilities with respect to the issue?

You can make decisions without knowing the law, but I don't recommend it. Divorce is a process governed by the law. You need to know the law in order to make fully informed decisions. For example, let's say your ex has a sizable interest in a long-standing family business. Let's say you don't realize that you have a legal claim to half of that value so you ignore the asset in your settlement. If you knew your legal rights, you still might decide not to enforce your claim and take your half. But you might, especially if it's worth big bucks! Make sure you know the law before you make decisions.

DIY Consideration #3: Do you have sufficient information with respect to the issue?

You don't know what you don't know so you might not be able to answer this question with certainty. Experienced professionals can help you with that, since they'll likely have seen similar situations. Huddle with your team for some information gathering before you decide to handle something on your own. Pay attention if they are nervous about your handling of a specific issue by yourself. Professionals are there to protect you and, sometimes, to protect you from yourself.

DIY Consideration #4: To what extent is the issue mixed up with other issues?

Beware of handling specific issues on your own if they are part of a bigger deal. Stick with standalone issues. For example, maybe you and your ex continue to jointly own the family recreation property and you want to divide up the summer months. Creating the schedule for property use directly with your ex is a low-risk proposition. If it's simple to separate the issue from the bigger picture, you might consider handling it on your own. Just promise me you'll be careful.

Choosing a Divorce Approach

People often begin their divorce in one of two camps.

There's the sweetness and light camp filled with people planning on consciously uncoupling without conflict and with minimal involvement from lawyers. They trust that their ex will be fair and they are committed to being fair with their ex. Maturity and enlightenment all 'round.

Then there's the scorched-earth camp filled with people who are angry, or scared, or both, and each wants to strike first. Typically, they each hire the toughest lawyers in town and pursue an aggressive campaign that often ends in court and always ends with loads of legal fees.

The most effective approach is more balanced. I'm all for sweetness and light. I'm all for cooperation and collaboration throughout the process. But keep in mind that if you ask ten people to describe a fair outcome in a specific divorce, odds are you will get ten different answers.

There is nothing wrong with the belief that your ex wants to be fair. That's great. But also accept that their definition of fair likely won't look exactly like yours. Know your rights, know the facts, be reasonable and professional while representing your interests. Maturity and enlightenment all 'round. And knowledge and pragmatism too.

As for the scorched-earth camp, I understand that you're angry, or scared, or both. But consider parking that fear and anger when you are deciding on the most effective approach to handling the business of your divorce.

With moderation in mind, let's talk about the various approaches to working through the business of your divorce. At the beginning of the process, you'll hear these terms swirling around: mediation, arbitration, litigation. Before we dig into those details, you'll need to choose an overall approach.

Divorce Approach #1: The collaborative process

There is a general dissatisfaction with the combative approach to the divorce process, at least among the people I work with, and maybe you too. People often begin their divorce with the hope of sorting it out like reasonable individuals. That well-intentioned motive is how the collaborative family law process was born over thirty years ago.

Here's how the collaborative process typically works:

- You and your ex each hire lawyers who practice collaborative family law.

- Individually, you might hire other advisers, like an accountant and a counselor.

- Jointly, you hire other technical advisers to help with the process, like valuators, appraisers, tax specialists, and whoever you may need.

- You both commit that you will not go to court. Instead, you will work toward a negotiated settlement.

- Your lawyers will employ various strategies to help you reach a deal: Facilitated meetings between you and your ex, lawyer-to-lawyer communication, mediation. Typically, anything and everything short of arbitration or litigation.
- If things fall apart, you and your ex must walk away from your lawyers and jointly engaged experts. None of them can continue to work for either of you.
- In the end, you'll either have a final settlement or you'll start from scratch in the traditional process.

The idea of collaborating to reach a negotiated settlement makes perfect sense to me. But keep in mind that there are some limitations to this process.

First, sometimes people need the "stick" of court as well as the "carrot" of a cheaper, faster, more civil process to motivate them to get a deal done. In the collaborative process, you don't have that stick.

Second, if things fall apart, you've lost some time and money since both you and your ex need to put together new advisory teams.

Divorce Approach #2: The traditional process

Even within the traditional process, you are free to be collaborative. But there is a key difference between the traditional and collaborative approaches. In the collaborative approach, collaboration is hard-wired into the system. There are penalties imposed if you decide that collaboration is no longer working, like the need to replace your advisory team.

Here's how the traditional process typically works:

- You and your ex each hire lawyers who practice family law.

- Individually, you might hire other advisers, like an accountant and a counselor.

- Jointly, you might engage other technical advisers to help with valuations and appraisals.

- You both hope (if you are well advised) that you will not go to court. Instead, you will work toward a negotiated settlement.

- Your lawyers will employ various strategies to help you reach a deal: facilitated meetings between you and your ex, lawyer-to-lawyer communication, mediation, arbitration, or litigation.

- In the end, you'll either have a negotiated or imposed final settlement.

Good lawyers will begin the process by familiarizing themselves with the material facts and then initiating a dialogue with your ex's team. Good lawyers and accountants will help you reach a negotiated settlement.

Guided Pathways

Regardless of your overall approach, concluding your divorce may require some form of third-party involvement. Maybe you and your ex, with the help of your respective teams, will reach a deal. But if you get stuck, here are the paths you can take to get un-stuck.

Pathway #1: Mediation

Sometimes negotiations stall out. For example, let's say you were making good progress... until your ex decided that they absolutely, positively must have every copy of every family photo and won't budge on the issue. Or until you decided that you couldn't stand the idea of giving up the cottage that's been in your ex's family for generations and you won't budge. Mediation can help people get un-stuck.

The term mediation covers all sorts of situations, ranging from a formal mediation process to an informal call from your friend to your ex's friend in an attempt to broker an agreement. However, the friends-calling-friends type of mediation gives me the same jitters that the you-doing-stuff-yourself idea gives me. If you are considering an informal mediation, please proceed with the same caution that I recommended when considering handling any part of your divorce yourself. Or just don't do it because I'm worried you'll strike a crappy or unenforceable deal.

Typically, in the formal version, mediation is a non-binding process in which a knowledgeable, impartial third party, often a family lawyer, works to help you and your ex find a mutually agreeable outcome. Well, let's say an outcome you can both live with. "Agreeable" isn't an appropriate description for divorce-related outcomes. Typically, both your and your ex's lawyers and accountants will be part of this process, helping to explain your position and advising you on any proposed solutions put forward by the mediator. The mediator is impartial because they don't represent your or your ex's interests. They just try to help you reach an agreement.

Searching for the right mediator is like searching for any other professional, so refer to the guidelines starting on page 98 to help you with your selection process. Also, since you will likely have assembled your core team in advance of engaging a mediator, request your team's help in making your choice.

Mediation shouldn't feel scary. The mediator's sole objective is to help you reach an agreement. You are still the decision-maker.

Pathway #2: Arbitration

Unfortunately, in some circumstances people can't reach a deal through negotiation or mediation. They need the help of a third-party decision-maker: either an arbitrator or a judge.

Arbitration looks like mediation but there is an important distinction: the arbitrator is the decision-maker, not you, and not your ex. In that respect, arbitration and litigation (carrying out a court proceeding) are close cousins. In both cases, you are handing over the authority to impose an outcome to a third party. I would only recommend going down the path of arbitration (or litigation; see next point) when you have reached an impasse and have given up on the possibility of working it out with your ex.

When you are negotiating, you are free to come up with any creative solutions that work for both of you. An arbitrator or a judge will be more likely to come up with mainstream solutions and it's unusual for anyone to come out feeling like a winner. More often, you'll both come out exhausted, disappointed, and poorer than when you went in.

Pathway #3: Litigation

You probably already have an idea about litigation, one that you've seen in the movies. But the movies don't give you a precise picture.

Litigation isn't just your day in court. Litigation is the court process, start to finish, from filing a motion and demanding financial disclosure from your ex all the way through to arguing your case in front of a judge. Just because you start a litigation doesn't mean you'll be going to trial. In fact, most divorce litigation ends in settlement before trial.

Be warned, litigation takes forever... or, at least, it seems like forever when it's your divorce. The wheels of justice turn slow—super-duper slow. It feels hard to even call it justice because often people feel exhausted as opposed to vindicated at the end of a litigation.

You might be wondering why anybody would litigate if it is slow, expensive, and uncertain. Good question. Unfortunately, there are times when two people can't reach an agreement on their own. Sometimes, when one person is being unreasonable, the only reasonable way to deal with them is to proceed with litigation. So although it isn't, or shouldn't be, your opening move, litigation may be necessary.

Choosing Your A-Team

Alrighty. You've decided on the type of professionals you need on your team and on your general approach. But how do you choose the right individuals? First, you'll need to do some research. Ask around for a good lawyer, accountant, and counselor. Ask friends and family who have been through divorce, ask other professionals you have worked with and respect, and, of course, ask Siri.

When you have a list of possible candidates, meet with those who resonate with you the most. Definitely interview more than one, even if you really like the first one. Take notes. Ask questions. Reflect. And bear the following guidelines in mind when making your choices.

Guideline #1: Price

Hire the best person you can afford. This isn't a time to find the cheapest service provider. However, you have to be practical. Talk about fees up front. If that makes you nervous, think of it as practice for the many tough conversations you will be having during this process.

If you've chosen well, your advisers will become an important part of your support system during your divorce. But remember, it's business. That doesn't mean they don't care about you. I care very much about my clients. The best lawyers I work with care very much about their clients. However, advisers wouldn't be in business for long if they didn't charge for their time. Don't take that personally.

Hourly rates are a function of supply and demand. Advisers with tons of experience, expertise, and proficiency in a large market typically have higher rates than those with less experience, expertise, and proficiency in smaller markets. Don't take that personally. The hourly rate was established before you came along and will live on when your divorce is finalized. It's up to you to determine whether the rate reflects good value and whether you can afford to pay.

Here are a few questions to ask about price:

1. What is your hourly rate?

2. Do you work with an associate or associates and, if so, what are their hourly rates?

3. Do you charge a retainer? (This is a type of upfront deposit.)

4. How often do you bill and when do you expect payment?

Guideline #2: Expertise

You want to be your advisers' typical client. You want them to have sufficient relevant experience that they aren't learning on your dime. And, clearly, you want them to be good at their job. I suggest reading all available marketing material, profiles, and publications related to their practice, and asking for references from their colleagues and former clients.

If you've decided on the traditional approach, there is another wrinkle to consider when it comes to your potential lawyer's expertise. Some lawyers aren't comfortable in a courtroom. That might be a surprise to you since, based on the movies, you might think that lawyers spend most of their time in a courtroom. Typically, in reality (boring compared to the movies), lawyers spend most of their time in their offices. Now, most people hope they won't end up in divorce court. But if you do end up in court and your lawyer isn't comfortable or experienced, you will be at a disadvantage. So, if you choose the traditional approach, you might want to choose a lawyer who can handle a courtroom.

Here are a few questions to ask your team about their expertise:

1 Can you describe your professional background?

2 How long have you been practicing?

3 Can you describe your typical client?

4 Can you describe your trial experience? (That one is just for lawyers.)

Guideline #3: Philosophy

Professionals are people, too, each with a different world view and philosophy. Although you choose your accountant mainly for their expertise with numbers and your lawyer for their expertise in the law, you'll also want to understand their world view because it informs their work. When you are choosing a counselor, it's particularly important to understand their perspectives and beliefs, since those beliefs are likely to influence the nature of their work with you.

Fortunately, counselors have a leg up here and should be comfortable discussing their life philosophy. But where lawyers and accountants are concerned, examining this criteria can be tricky as many might not be able to clearly answer questions about their overarching view of the world.

I'll give you an example. When it comes to choosing your lawyer, ask yourself this: do I want a lover or a fighter? Wait, don't turn your lawyer into your lover. You know what I mean. It's common to wonder whether you would get a better deal and stick it to your ex in the process if you hire a warrior-type lawyer. Unless you like the idea of war, I do not recommend hiring a warrior, even though I completely understand the temptation.

Maybe you're mad and want someone to fight for you. Maybe you're scared and want someone to protect you. Maybe you think that you'll end up with a bigger share of the pie if you launch an offensive. But, in my experience, the lawyers that profile themselves as warriors are less effective. Your lawyer should be confident, competent, and assertive, yes. Full of bluster and bravado, no. In my experience, bluster and bravado mask a lack of confidence and competence.

What if your ex hires a warrior? You might think that you need to follow suit. You might think that rational advisers who are focused on finding a resolution would be steamrolled by warriors. That isn't my experience. In my experience, dueling warriors means more suffering and a smaller pie to divide as you and your ex both fund the battle.

It's important to make sure that your professional's philosophies align with yours.

Here are a few questions to ask about philosophy:

1 Can you describe your general approach and style?

2 How do you handle conflict?

3 What is your strategy in a negotiation? (To ask potential lawyers and accountants.)

4 How many of your divorce files proceed to litigation? (This one is just for lawyers.)

Guideline #4: The human element

The human element is crucial to consider when you are looking for your divorce team. Here are the issues to bear in mind when selecting those professionals who are going to be with you on your divorce journey.

Don't hire a friend. The more dispassionate you and your advisers can be in this process, the better. Friends are likely to increase your emotional temperature and lower your boundaries. This can work against you, as healthy boundaries and a low emotional temperature are key to your success.

Hire people you understand. If it seems like they are speaking another language when they explain the technical issues, then their advice will be useless. This isn't rocket science, so if a lawyer or accountant leaves your head spinning, best to find another one.

Hire someone who shows you respect. Sure, they are experts in their field. That's why you want to hire them. But that doesn't make them better than you. If they are under the mistaken impression that it does, don't hire them. Hire professionals who increase your self-confidence—who build you up, not tear you down.

Hire someone you respect. You don't want to second guess the advice you receive. Respect is an intangible quality, but you know it if you feel it. There is a cocktail of many things that lead to a professional gaining your respect. In the end this is a question of gut-feel: do they calm your butterflies or start them flapping?

Hire advisers who work well with others. The divorce-advisory circle is pretty small in many locales. Professionals who have made divorce their focus tend to know those other professionals who are in the same line of work. Certain advisers develop a reputation for being unreasonable, or for lacking the necessary expertise, or for being plain unfriendly. You don't want the personality or approach of your advisers to become a barrier to wrapping up your divorce, so gather information about a potential adviser's reputation and relationships with other professionals before making your final choice. Ask for references from colleagues. And, simply put, consider whether or not they are likable.

Guideline #5: Specialization

Most professionals choose a specific type of work for a specific type of client because it's hard to be all things to all people. In our complex modern world, high-quality generalists are few and far between so beware the professional who claims to be one. Make sure you choose a professional with the specialization that matches your needs. I'll give you a few examples.

There are lawyers who are unbiased and those who are biased. The unbiased types are mediators, arbitrators, and, ultimately, judges. When you are assembling your team, I recommend hiring the biased type because you need help with understanding your legal position, developing your legal strategy, and figuring out when or if you need to engage one of the unbiased types of lawyers. Remember, if you choose the collaborative process, then you'll need a lawyer who practices in that field.

Similarly, there are accountants who are unbiased, "expert-witness" types, like valuators, appraisers, and forensic specialists. These expert witnesses often work for both you and your ex. Their job is to provide unbiased opinions to help you reach a negotiated settlement or to provide a basis for a judgment in a litigation. Then there are those who are biased: the advocates. Advocates are partial to their clients. When you are assembling your initial team, I recommend hiring the type of accountant who is partial to you. The partial types will help you develop your financial strategy and figure out when, or if, you need to engage one of those expert-witness type of accountants.

Here's where it gets tricky. You might find a family lawyer who practices in both the collaborative and traditional approach. You might find an expert-witness type of accountant who will happily work as your advocate. So, let's simplify things: when you assemble your core team, look for professionals who specialize in being advocates because you need people who are solidly in your corner.

Here are a few questions to ask about specialization:

1. Would you work for me as an advocate, or are you impartial?
2. Is your practice specialized and, if so, can you describe your specialty?
3. Do you practice collaborative or traditional family law, or both? (This is for lawyers.)

Managing Your Team

You've chosen your approach. You've assembled your team. And now you need to embrace your role as team leader. Here are some things to keep in mind to ensure that your team functions well and you are a good boss. Happily, managing your team well also saves you money.

What follows are my suggestions for managing your team like a good boss.

Boss Tip #1: Lead, don't follow

A good leader knows that they don't have all the answers. You probably aren't an expert in divorce, so it makes sense that you won't have all the answers. After all, you've assembled your team for exactly that reason. But here's the thing: you do have to make all the big decisions—you can't abdicate this. Don't worry, you should be well supported in this process. Your professionals will guide you, advise you, and take care of the technical work. Your job is to consider their advice and make decisions.

Your ability to be decisive and stick with your decisions will be one of the most important ways in which you can improve the efficiency of your divorce (a.k.a. minimize fees!). Now, you're human and this is divorce, so don't beat yourself up if you do some flip-flopping. Also, you will want to remain flexible throughout the process as you gain more information and proceed with negotiations. But, as much as possible, make decisions carefully and stick with 'em. Proceeding with the methodical planning process that we'll review in part two will help.

Boss Tip #2: Communication is key

If you don't have a ton of experience leading a team, you might underestimate the impact you have as leader. But trust me, your communication will have a big impact on your divorce team. It's super important for all members of the team to be well informed. When you're paying people by the hour, it is natural that you might feel anxious about keeping everyone informed. The trick is to avoid wasting time—and incomplete information or miscommunication leads to wasted time.

Here are some ways to avoid that trap:

1. Clearly communicate your expectations.

2. Listen carefully to your team.

3. Provide professional, constructive feedback, politely. Remember, divorce professionals are people, too, so be kind when sharing any "opportunities for growth."

4. Be generous with positive feedback, and the more specific, the better. Your team will work harder for you if they feel appreciated.

5. Develop a communication approach with your team to establish preferred methods of communication (email, text, phone, or in-person), frequency and timing of communication (work hours, workdays, and scheduled updates), and the type of information that should be exchanged (and with whom).

Boss Tip #3: Pick a point person

Your divorce team is going to need a point person. Your point person, or spokesperson, is responsible for communicating with "the other side"—your ex's side. Appointing one clear point person will minimize miscommunication from mixed messages, improve adherence to the strategy or plan, and lower your emotional temperature during the process.

Often, this point person will be your lawyer, and occasionally they will be your accountant. But almost never will the point person be you. To be clear, the point person isn't the boss. You are the boss. The point person is just out front interfacing with your ex's point person.

Your ex or their team members might try to deal directly with you or another member of your team and go around your point person. But be a good team leader and send them back to talk to the point person. You'll avoid mixed messages, which at best waste time and at worst compromise your negotiating position.

Boss Tip #4: Address billing concerns politely

Getting divorced is expensive. Unfortunately, you will likely need to spend a painful amount of money to get it done. Don't expect to enjoy receiving the invoices for professional fees, but do expect to feel like it is money wisely spent. During the process, continue to assess the value of your advisers' work. Are they worth the price?

One key consideration with respect to the value offered by your lawyer or accountant is the pace of progress in your divorce. The longer it takes, the more expensive it will be. The more your advisers have to put down and pick up your file, the more time they will spend re-educating themselves on the facts of your case, and that costs you money.

Given that divorce takes two, it may be that slow progress is not the responsibility of your team but an outcome of the slow pace set by your ex and their team. Stay informed with respect to the source of delays. How long does it take your team to respond to you? How quickly do they get work done when the ball is in their court?

You have every right to voice any concerns you may have with respect to billing. So, if you do begin to doubt the value proposition, raise the issue politely. Raging at your lawyer or accountant or counselor about their bills will not be well received. The professional services community is small, so behavior like that might make it hard to find a replacement.

Boss Tip #5: Continuously evaluate your team's performance

Continuous performance evaluation is critical, but be cautious when doing this. Divorce sucks and you can expect to feel unhappy and anxious during the process. Sometimes, that general unhappiness and anxiety might lead you to question whether or not you have the right professionals on your team. You have to work to be pragmatic in your assessment. Try to isolate the performance of your team from your general divorce unhappiness. It's perfectly normal to be dissatisfied with the process. The process sucks. But think carefully before concluding that it's your advisers who suck.

Please tread carefully when soliciting second opinions. But if you do ask other professionals for a second opinion, ensure they don't have a conflict of interest. If they want your business, they might be inclined toward negativity about your existing team. Also, make sure you are painting a complete picture on which they can form their second opinion. As they say, the devil is in the details. So make sure you share sufficient information about your divorce. And, pretty please, do not rely on your friends for a second opinion. Divorce is like parenting: everybody has opinions and advice, whether you want it or not. Remember that every divorce is unique and what worked for your friends might not work for you.

Boss Tip #6: Switch advisers with caution

If you find yourself in the unfortunate situation where you want to fire one of your advisers, please think very carefully. Switching advisers involves additional cost and time. Your former and new adviser will need to communicate. Your new adviser will need to invest time to get up to speed on your case. That time is gonna cost you.

A Quick Summary

- Understand the nature of your marriage to understand the help you'll need during your divorce.

- Your divorce team should consist of a lawyer, an accountant, and a counselor.

- Choose a divorce approach that best matches your needs.

- When choosing professionals, consider their price, expertise, philosophy, and specialization.

- When managing your team, remember: you are the boss.

TWO

PROTECTING YOUR FINANCIAL HEALTH

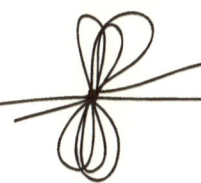

5

Managing Divorce Limbo

Financial security *during* your divorce is vital.

A LL RIGHT, you and your team are ready to do this divorce. Let the games begin. Wait. No. Let the work begin. We are wading into the hard labor of divorce. I will do everything in my power to minimize the soul-crushing aspects of this part of the preparation process. You are not alone if you have a sense of dread when you contemplate sifting through paperwork and crunching numbers. But I guarantee, like most things you dread, it isn't as bad as you imagine. Let's dig in and get it done so you can get on with your life.

I know: wouldn't it be lovely if you could just push a button and your and your ex's finances would immediately divide without a fuss? I suppose I'd be reimagining my career, but it would still be lovely. In reality, the process of unraveling your financial connection with your ex can take a long time, sometimes years.

Sure, things are probably going to move along at a decent pace if you are thirty years old and have next to no money and next to no income, as I was in my first divorce. But if you've been married for thirty years and have loads of money and income, getting divorced can take years. I hate telling you this, but it's important: you need to make sure that you are financially safe and secure while you are working through the process of divorce.

Let's call the time between your initial separation and reaching a final settlement "divorce limbo." Filled with change and uncertainty, divorce limbo is a strange purgatory between being married and being divorced. Sometimes you feel like things are moving so fast your head is spinning. Sometimes you feel like nothing is progressing and you want to scream with frustration. Divorce limbo sucks. And since everyone wants to get through it as quickly as possible, it's tempting to focus immediately on the work of sorting out your final settlement. But don't.

If you don't have any money during divorce limbo and you can't buy groceries, then you won't be able to work on your final settlement because you'll die of starvation. And even if you don't die, worrying that you might die of starvation during your divorce limbo will mean that you are negotiating from a weak position (hello, low blood sugar). You will be desperate to reach an agreement even if the terms suck. At a bare minimum, you need to address your survival needs with a limbo plan. Better yet, shoot for thriving, not just surviving.

Maybe you're thinking, "I don't need a limbo plan, things are fine, my ex and I are managing our finances the way we managed them during our marriage." That's when I break into a cold sweat, because I've heard that before and it rarely goes smoothly. The road to your final

settlement is likely to be bumpy, and those bumps have a way of disrupting financial arrangements that rely on everyone getting along.

Doing the Limbo

Let me warn you now: this stage is often one of the bumpiest financial roads in the divorce journey. Often the law is vague with respect to divorce limbo, and people are in the early stages of a traumatic experience. Boundaries are low, emotions are high, and advisers are either new or nonexistent. Buckle up and wear a helmet.

Before we dig into the financial nitty-gritty, here are the most important considerations when you are establishing your limbo plan.

Limbo Prep #1: Plan early

The purpose of a limbo plan is to protect you. But it is much harder to get a limbo plan in place after your ex has decided to close the joint account and cancel the credit card. Let's err on the side of caution and get that plan in place before you, say, start dating a new love interest. I'd rather that you have protection you don't need than no protection when you need it. Let's hope for the best and plan for the worst, said every accountant about everything.

Limbo Prep #2: Protect your finances

Your limbo plan provides you with financial security. Well, let me rephrase that: you'll have more financial security with a limbo plan than without. Divorce involves financial instability: your financial apple cart has been overturned and apples are flying everywhere. Still, we are looking to get you as much security as possible so that you can work toward your divorce deal without feeling desperate.

Although the familiarity of status quo might feel safe, it is not safe if your ex can make unilateral changes that hurt you. Please do not accept the financial status quo, especially if it requires that you rely on the generous spirit of your ex.

Let's say that, during your marriage, your ex was the breadwinner and managed the family finances. In the early days of your separation, you continued to have unrestricted access to the joint bank account and credit cards. Your ex continued to deposit their paycheck into the joint account. Fast forward three months. Your independence and self-esteem are on the rise and you've started dating. Your ex struggles with those changes, stops depositing the paycheck, and cancels the joint credit card.

If your divorce starts with the shell-shocked or hopeful-for-reconciliation stage, you and your ex might not make a ton of changes to your finances. If your divorce starts with the fury and hate stage, freezing accounts or binge spending might ensue. I know that you won't use money as a weapon in your divorce, but be prepared that your ex may not be as enlightened.

Limbo Prep #3: Use teamwork

Even though I want you to get your limbo plan in place as soon as possible, don't rush. While you might be thinking this is one of those somethings that you can do yourself, I recommend that you rely on the expertise of your team. Since this is one of the issues that you'll tackle first, your nerves are likely frayed and you might not be thinking clearly. I'm worried that you'll agree to something you'll regret or inadvertently compromise your legal position. Your limbo plan should be a team effort.

Limbo Prep #4: Make it official

Remember, one of the key goals of establishing a limbo plan is to provide you with financial security. Let's not base your security on a handshake. Let's make it official. There are a number of ways to do this, ranging from something as simple as outlining the deal in an email exchange with your ex to executing a legal agreement to getting a court order. Choosing the right level of formality should also be a team effort. You'll need to consider the nature of your relationship and the complexity of your situation when making your choice. Wherever you land, just make sure that you aren't at the mercy of your ex's good graces. Let's protect you with something in writing.

Limbo Prep #5: Beware nervous bankers

A good relationship with your banker is a valuable thing. Your banker can make sure you have access to cash in a pinch. Your banker can arrange the mortgage for that great little cottage at the beach. Your banker can get you the credit card with the super high limit. Or not.

A solid relationship with your banker is something you might not value until it's gone. You might not even notice that your relationship with your banker has gone down the toilet until you are in a financial bind and they won't help.

That's why I'm reminding you that bankers get nervous when people get divorced. They worry that you won't pay your debts. They worry about getting caught in the legal middle. Nervous bankers do things like remove your access to lines of credit, cut your limits on your credit cards, think twice before renewing your mortgage, and freeze access to your accounts.

Sure, you can always switch banks. But the best time to switch banks is when you don't need to. Bankers can smell desperation. When a banker smells desperation, interest rates go up and access to financing goes down. Your desperation makes them nervous.

How do you calm the nerves of your banker? You exude calm. Bankers are like dogs. I love dogs, so I mean this as a compliment. When you are nervous, they are nervous. When you are calm, they are calm. Never, ever share your divorce dramas with your banker. Stick with the facts. Never lie, just avoid negativity. And, best of all, come up with a clear limbo plan. Bankers love plans. They love it when their clients take the initiative to come up with plans. You know what they say: "Happy banker, happy life." And, if all else fails, you can try CBD drops.

Limbo Prep #6: Guard your liquidity

Liquidity is your ability to get your hands on cash, fast. Liquidity is always important. But it's even more important during times of uncertainty and change. Times when you might need to pack a bag, grab all your cash, and leave town in the middle of the night. No, I'm kidding. I don't think that will be necessary. But when times are uncertain, you do want the ability to deal with whatever challenges come your way. That might be coping with an interruption in your income, or needing to furnish your new place, or paying legal bills.

Decision-Making: Who's in Charge?

Now let's dig into the nitty-gritty. When you're married, it's common to divide and conquer and focus on your strengths. They mowed the lawn and you did the laundry. They washed the car and you cleaned the toilets. I don't know about you, but I think I'd rather mow the lawn and wash the car. Part of your job during divorce limbo is to learn or relearn all those things that your ex handled during your marriage. Have faith that this will happen, just not overnight.

Sometimes, the dividing and conquering strategy applies to the family finances. Maybe you were the financial manager. Maybe your ex was the financial manager. Either way, during divorce limbo it's important that major decisions are made jointly. Your financial interests are no longer naturally aligned through marriage. That means you shouldn't delegate financial decision-making to one person.

Let's say that during your marriage, management of the finances looked like this:

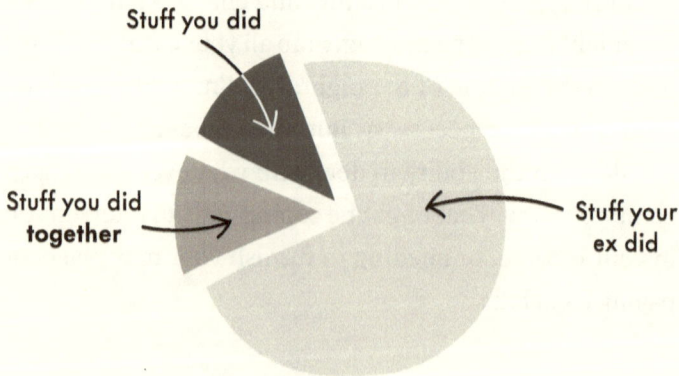

During limbo, management of your finances should look more like this:

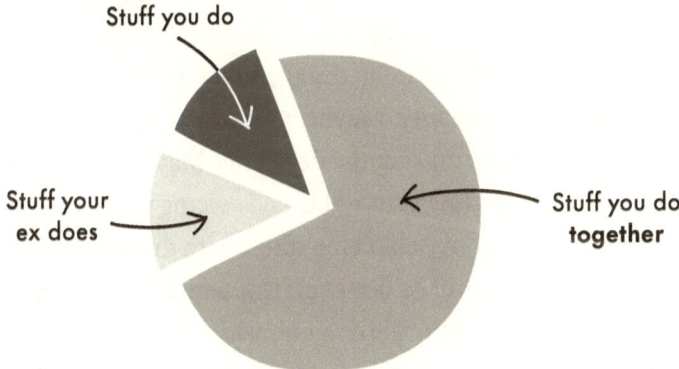

Strange, huh? Now that you are separated, you should make more decisions together. To give you something to look forward to, here is the light at the end of the tunnel:

But you've got some work to do before you get there.

In the meantime, if you are the person who used to make all the decisions, you have a hard habit to break. Now you'll have to start involving your ex in financial decision-making. If you are the person who allowed your ex to make all the decisions, you also have a hard habit to break. Because now you've got to start participating in financial decision-making.

Some people have to be dragged kicking and screaming into this new reality. Maybe your ex is a control freak who wants to keep making the decisions. Maybe you aren't comfortable asserting your rights and voicing your opinion. As a change-hater myself, I empathize with that resistance. But trust me, you will be better off if you make this change.

In practice, some people don't transition to joint decision-making at all. They just carry on making decisions that affect one another with reckless abandon. But disregarding joint decision-making on joint stuff is a speedy way to derail the business of your divorce. Selling the antique car collection that your ex spent twenty years accumulating might give you some momentary devilish glee. Buying another antique car that drains your joint bank account might give them some momentary devilish glee. But blood boiling will ensue. Not a solid foundation on which to build a successful negotiation and good settlement. Hello, derailing.

Financial Decisions You Should Make on Your Own

Now, let's get specific about what decisions you should make on your own. There are two categories for this type of decision.

Solo Decision #1: Day-to-day spending

It would be impractical and inappropriate for you to weigh in on each other's day-to-day spending decisions. Heck, it's not even appropriate for you to *know* about each other's day-to-day spending. Spending provides a life road map: where you go and what you do. And even though this new reality often takes some getting used to, your daily spending isn't one another's business anymore.

You might be worried about each other's spending. That's natural. But the answer is not calling one another every time you buy groceries or a new pair of shoes. That's impractical and inappropriate.

Solo Decision #2: Excluded property

It is possible that you each have stuff that isn't part of the shared pie. You must be careful here because sometimes you and your ex might have a different opinion about what stuff is and is not part of the shared pie. You absolutely, positively need help on this one.

If you determine there are things that aren't part of the shared pie, then you don't need to make shared decisions about those things. Let's call this stuff "excluded property." For example, let's say that you inherited a cottage from your grandma. Let's say the law in your location is that you get to keep it and not include it in the shared pie. That means you can make decisions about that property without consulting your ex.

Financial Decisions You Should Make Together

Since your finances are still intertwined at this point, we need to look at the financial decisions you will have to make together. There are three categories for this type of decision.

Joint Decision #1: Big spending

First, you'll need to decide what "big spending" means to you. Big spending is infrequent and has a major impact on your finances. Since it's infrequent, it's practical and appropriate for both of you to weigh in on big spending decisions. Big spending has major impact, so it can derail the process if either of you go it alone.

Joint Decision #2: Joint spending

Especially when you are in the early stages of divorce limbo, it's likely that you will continue to have shared obligations with your ex. This might be spending on your kids, or to maintain shared property, or for shared loan payments. Decisions regarding joint spending should be joint (I'm guessing that one was obvious).

Joint Decision #3: Family property

Family property is all the stuff you share until you have a final settlement. And that isn't necessarily just the stuff that has both your and your ex's name on it. Don't get mixed up on the difference between *legal* ownership and *beneficial* ownership.

Legal ownership refers to the person with their name on the property, legally. Let's say your ex is the only person "on title" of the family home. If you go to your local land title registry and ask who owns the home, they'll tell you that your ex owns it. They are the legal owner. Their name is on title. Let's say your ex owns a company and they are the only shareholder. If you ask your local corporate registrar who owns the company, they'll tell you that your ex owns the company. They are the legal owner, the holder of shares.

However, it is possible that the family home and the company can be considered shared family property because you and your ex are both *beneficial* owners of that home or that company. In the long run, beneficial ownership is more important than legal ownership. But in the short run, legal owners might have more decision-making control, because the rest of the world assumes they are just plain "owners." Do you see how people can get mixed up over this?

Let's boil it down to this: the type of ownership that matters for your joint decision-making is beneficial ownership. Family property is the stuff that you and your ex beneficially own together.

Figuring Out Your Ground Rules

Now that you know what financial decisions you need to make on your own and what decisions you need to share, let's talk about how you are going to handle those shared decisions.

Far better to figure out your ground rules before disaster strikes, as in before your ex takes on a bunch more debt, for which you are also on the hook, or drains your investments to buy a boat. You'll need to establish a decision-making framework. That sounds fancy, but it isn't. It can be, and should be, super simple. Frankly, it's just about creating some rules for spending and managing your shared stuff. Lists and rules. I'm in heaven.

What follows are some ideas for ground rules to get the ball rolling. Feel free to pick other ground rules that fit your situation. Just make sure that you pick some, because financial management during divorce limbo without ground rules can be a bit like the wild west without a sheriff in town.

Rule Set #1: The big spending

Put a number on it. Maybe for you it's $100 or $1,000 or $10,000. It's personal and relative to your wealth. It isn't the number that matters. What matters is that you and your ex come to an agreement on what the "big" in big spending means to you.

Here are some examples of big spending ground rules:

Ground Rule 1: Spending over $5,000 is big spending.

Ground Rule 2: We will discuss big spending in advance.

Ground Rule 3: If you don't agree with my big spending plan, I will either wait until after our final settlement or I'll use my own money, not from the shared stuff pile. If I don't agree with your big spending plan, you will either wait until after our final settlement or use your own money.

Rule Set #2: Your joint spending

You'll need to get clear about what spending is joint. Simply put, if you are splitting the cost, it's joint spending. Since this spending can be significant in the early days of limbo, it's useful to get specific. Make a list. Post it on the fridge. It will be a helpful reminder to consult your ex before you buy junior that new set of golf clubs.

Here are some examples of joint spending ground rules:

Ground Rule 1: We will establish a budget for our joint spending.

Ground Rule 2: We will discuss deviations from that budget in advance.

Ground Rule 3: If you don't agree with my joint spending deviation, I'll use my own money. If I don't agree with your joint spending deviation, you will use your own money.

Ground Rule 4: We'll each deposit 50 percent of our joint spending budget into a specified bank account every month.

Don't freak out about that last one. We'll talk about where you'll get the cash later. Maybe your ex will fund all joint spending. Maybe you'll use your savings. We'll figure it out starting on page 142.

Rule Set #3: Your family property

Remember, family property is stuff that both of you beneficially own. You need ground rules to ensure that neither you nor your ex are making changes to your stuff without one another's knowledge or consent.

Now, there might be small issues related to your family property that only one of you need handle. For example, you take your car in for repairs or buy new snow tires. Or your ex makes the payment on your shared credit card. You want to be practical about these smaller issues because you don't want the obligation of making insignificant decisions jointly.

But you do want to make significant decisions together, such as putting a new roof on the cabin, investing in your ex-brother-in-law's start-up company, or selling your car because you're always taking it in for repairs.

Here are some examples of family property ground rules:

Ground Rule 1: Changes to family property over $5,000 are significant.

Ground Rule 2: We will discuss significant changes to family property in advance.

Ground Rule 3: If you don't agree with my family property plan, I will wait until after our final settlement and then do what I want with my stuff. If I don't agree with your family property plan, you will wait until after our final settlement and then do what you want with your stuff.

Ground Rule 4: If we can't agree on significant changes, we will select the alternative that most closely resembles the status quo.

Following (or Enforcing) the Rules

Let's say that, after some grief, you've established ground rules. Great! But what do you do if your ex has trouble following the rules? Here are a few strategies.

Enforcer #1: Use your banker

You might be able to use your banker to enforce the rules. Of course, you don't want to make them nervous, so tread carefully.

If you have savings accounts, investment accounts, lines of credit, loans, or mortgages that are part of your shared stuff, consider converting those accounts to joint accounts if they aren't already. Now you might be wondering why you'd want to add your name to the line of credit. Here's why.

If your name is on something, you have easily enforceable rights. Since we're talking about the shared stuff, you're already on the hook for that line of credit. If your name isn't on the line of credit, then you have no easily enforceable way of controlling it. That would mean your ex could max it out to pay for the new boat and you'd be left trying to clean up the spilled milk. Better to have your hands on the milk jug so you can prevent it from spilling.

Once you have both of your names on it, you've got a way to enforce joint decision-making. You can let your banker know that all transactions require approval by both of you. Boom. Rules enforced.

A word of warning, however: there are some risks with this approach. What happens if you and your ex can't agree? Deadlock. Because you told the bank to do nothing unless an action is approved by both of you. No agreement, no action. Also, this approach is not practical for accounts that have a bunch of day-to-day activity. You don't want to be calling your ex to approve your grocery purchases.

Enforcer #2: Eliminate joint stuff if possible

I just advised putting your name on any financial obligations so you can enforce joint decision-making. However, if your finances permit, consider eliminating joint debt and spending obligations altogether to reduce your risk: close the joint line of credit, cancel the joint credit card, and terminate joint memberships and subscriptions. That's because you and your ex are typically both on the hook for those obligations.

You might be able to argue successfully in court that your ex is responsible for the cost of that private jet to Vegas with their new love interest. But that won't help you when your credit card is maxed out and you're fielding collection calls.

Just be careful. Remember the importance of liquidity, the ability to get your hands on cash. Don't pay off joint debt if it would mean that you have no cash.

If the timing makes financial sense, consider selling joint assets, as long as the market conditions are in your favor. Better to sell into a hot market with high prices. But be sure that you absolutely positively don't want to keep the asset in question. Sometimes, the immediate reaction to marriage breakdown is to clear the decks of any and all reminders of married life, like the family cottage where you enjoyed idyllic summers. As the dust settles, you might discover you actually do want to keep that cottage and make new summer memories.

Enforcer #3: Stabilize your finances

Once you have simplified your joint finances as much as prudently possible, keep your finances as stable as you can. Avoid major buying decisions or taking on a bunch of new debt. Clearly, these are change-filled days and you won't be able to strictly maintain the status quo. However, do what you can to minimize big changes that require big decisions.

Creating Your Spending Plan

Now let's get nittier and grittier. It's time to sort out your spending plan. How much will you be spending during divorce limbo and where will the money come from to cover that spending? I know that the word "budgeting" makes even the sanest among us cringe. Sorry about this, but you gotta do it. But remember what I said: it won't be as bad as you imagine. I hope. Either way, let's get to it.

We'll start with your spending. Not your ex's spending, not joint spending, just yours. Happily, this budget doesn't have to be fancy. We're talking one page.

Spending Factor #1: What are you spending now?

When it comes to establishing a financial budget or plan, it makes sense to understand your current spending and adjust for planned changes rather than start from scratch. That means your first step is to figure out your current spending.

You're not alone if you have no idea how much money you spend. Not to worry: it isn't all that tough to figure out. If you do most of your spending using a credit card, you're in luck. Most credit card statements have categorized spending summaries. But if that doesn't do the trick, you'll need to work a bit harder. You'll need to track your spending.

Review your bank statements and prepare a simple spreadsheet to categorize your spending. If you're saying "no bloody way," perhaps get your accountant to take care of that for you. Either way, you've got to get it done because while you might think you spend $500 a month on dinners out, a little tracking work might reveal that you actually spend $1,500. Reviewing your real spending will help you improve the accuracy of your limbo budget.

I feel like one of those personal trainers telling you to work out at five a.m. every morning. I'm worried that you won't do it. I'm trying to be realistic here. So, do your best to gather information on your existing spending. If you're up to it, track all your spending for a few months. If not, take your best guess.

Spending Factor #2: What is your limbo lifestyle?

Once you have a sense of your current spending, you'll need to figure out how your spending is going to change during your divorce limbo. That means you'll need to have an idea about what your life is going to look like. I get that your entire life has just turned on its ear and figuring out what it's going to look like might seem impossible, so let's set the bar a little lower. Just figure out a rough idea of your divorce limbo life. I hope you find it comforting to know that your divorce limbo life does not represent your post-divorce future. We'll get to that later.

Typically, the biggest limbo lifestyle question to answer is your living arrangement. Don't worry too much if your limbo home isn't something you would post on your vision board. Limbo won't last forever. That said, it's important that you feel safe, secure, and satisfied with your home. Remember, limbo can last a long time and you don't want to feel desperate to get it over with. A dark, damp basement suite from which you badly want to escape won't be a solid foundation on which to build a good negotiated settlement.

If you are the primary caregiver of kids, maybe it makes sense for you to stay in the family home while your ex rents an apartment close by. If you are empty nesters in a rental apartment, maybe it makes sense for each of you to rent smaller apartments. If you have a number of properties, maybe you could allocate one property to each of you as your limbo homes.

If at all possible, please do not continue to cohabitate. If you are considering cohabitating, even though I asked you not to, let me paint a picture to explain why I hate the idea. Things have been moving along wonderfully. Sweetness and light. Maturity and enlightenment. Then you start dating and, all of a sudden, things are worse than when you were a teenager and your dad met your dates at the door for a stern discussion about curfew. Now it's your ex meeting your dates at the door. Awkward. At that moment, the emotional aspect of divorce limbo comes crashing into the business aspect of divorce limbo and derails your negotiation. Instead of feeling safe, secure, and satisfied in your home, you feel like hiding in the guest bedroom and using the window as your front door. This is not a solid foundation on which to build a good negotiated settlement.

Spending Factor #3: Can you adjust your lifestyle?

Once you've sorted out your living arrangements, consider the rest of your lifestyle. Be prepared that establishing separate households typically means higher combined expenses. Unless you're wealthy, you may need to get creative to manage the resulting financial constraints.

When I was separated from my second husband, I had to reduce my spending. I am committed to fitness and, at the time of my separation, I had a conditioning trainer, a swim coach, and a triathlon coach—a team I could no longer afford. I cleared the decks. Yes, there was certainly some loss associated with that change, but also some unexpected benefits. My life was simpler, and I discovered that I have the discipline to pursue my fitness goals without an army. You might need to get creative in order to find savings.

Setting Your Limbo Budgets

With the information you've gathered on your current spending and a reasonable plan about the changes you'll be making during divorce limbo, you'll be ready to prepare your budgets—yours, and the one you will be managing with your ex.

Limbo Budget #1: Your spending

Remember, this first budget is just your spending. Your ex will be spending and you may have some joint spending (which we will discuss next), but let's start with just yours.

Here's an example of a personal budget:

Rent	$ 2,500
Groceries/meals	1,000
Utilities/phone/internet	800
Transportation/parking	750
Clothing/toiletries	500
Medical/dental	500
Entertainment/gifts	350
Your monthly spending	**$ 6,400**

Done. That wasn't so bad, right?!

In case you are worried about where the money is coming from to pay for your spending: we're getting there. One step at a time. When you are going through divorce, your fear will often be pointing out how scary the next step is. But you will suffer less if you can focus on the task at hand and worry about the next step when you are taking said next step.

For now, you're on a roll. So let's move on to your next list!

Limbo Budget #2: Your joint spending

Now let's budget your joint spending. This budget should be super simple. Joint spending is typically not new stuff. It's stuff you've been spending during your marriage that has continued into divorce limbo. It's the kids' expenses or the mortgage payment on the family home. Again, for now, don't worry about how you'll be paying for this joint stuff. This step is simply figuring out the amount of your joint spending obligations.

Here's an example of a joint budget:

Kids' tuition	$ 500
Kids' clothes	200
Kids' sports	350
Club memberships	100
Shared data plan (but please don't share a data plan)	100
Joint monthly spending	**$ 1,250**

Excellent! Now you know how much cash you'll need on a monthly basis during your divorce limbo. It's time to figure out where that cash will come from.

Finding the Money

When it comes to money coming in to pay for your limbo spending, there are only a few options:

1 Your or your ex's income.

2 Your stuff, your ex's stuff, or your shared stuff (a.k.a. assets).

3 Your borrowing, your ex's borrowing, or your joint borrowing (a.k.a. debt).

Let's pause here for a moment. Limbo planning is short-term planning (well, since I've already warned you that limbo can last an uncomfortably long time, let's call it short-ish-term planning). Postdivorce planning is long-term planning. It may be that you and your ex will spend more than you earn during limbo. And, as your accountant, I would tell you that this isn't a great long-term strategy. But you're in limbo, and things are up in the air. Of course, if you can't come up with the cash to cover your spending, you'll have to modify your lifestyle. But if you need to dip into some savings, sell some investments, or borrow from mom and dad to cover a small-ish shortfall, that isn't the end of the world.

Let's get back to those three sources of cash you can access to cover your spending.

Cash Source #1: Income

Maybe you work and earn sufficient cash to cover your spending. Super. That doesn't mean you shouldn't push for the support to which you are entitled. It just means that, during limbo, you will be financially safe and secure. Working through the issue of support is one of those tricky issues. You will definitely need to deal with it, and it's a relief to know that you can deal with it on the foundation of financial security. One issue to keep in mind is the possibility that you may be obligated to pay support to your ex. If you are obligated to pay support, you'll have to work that into your spending budget.

However, maybe your ex has been the main breadwinner. Maybe you quit work to take care of the kids. Maybe your current earnings aren't sufficient to cover your spending. In these cases, you'll need to address the issue of support during limbo. Let's call that "interim support." Interim support might look different from the support in your final settlement. It may be more or less.

Figuring out the issue of interim support is not one of those somethings you can or should do yourself. You'll need help to figure out a reasonable expectation and, likely, to encourage your ex to pay if they are obligated. Even if your ex is a saint, getting their head around a support obligation might be a challenge. Have patience, but don't relent. You need to be able to cover your living expenses during limbo. And if they have an obligation to pay, they should pay.

Cash Source #2: Assets

If your earnings combined with your interim support don't cover your spending, then you've got a few choices. First, you can spend less. But let's assume that you've cut your spending as much as humanly possible. What then?

The first of the two options you can use to cover that shortfall is your assets. I know that it sucks, but this might be one of those rainy days that you've been saving for. You might need to dip into your savings account to cover some of your spending. Financially speaking, divorce often includes taking a few steps back. Hopefully, only in the short term. I don't want you to be hard on yourself if you find yourself eating into your net worth a bit during your divorce limbo. You can focus on rebuilding when you've made it out the other side.

If that savings account is yours and yours alone, then you're in a position to make an independent decision about using some of that cash. But remember: if that savings account is a family asset, then this will be one of those joint decisions.

Cash Source #3: Debt

Your second option for covering a shortfall is to borrow money. Maybe you have a line of credit at the bank, or maybe you can get a new loan. Just remember what I told you about nervous bankers. It might be more difficult to convince your banker to loan you money when you are going through a divorce. Or maybe your ex isn't keen on running up the joint line of credit to cover your spending.

You can also consider asking for help from friends and family. I know, I know, you haven't asked your parents for money since you were twenty-two. That's why I'm putting this option at the bottom of the list. You've cut your spending as much as you can, you're earning as much as you can, you've pushed for any support to which you're entitled, you don't have any cash, and the bank won't loan you money. Time to call Mom and Dad. Or maybe your sister. I called my sister, and she helped me through my limbo.

Keep Your Powder Dry (a.k.a Plan for Disaster)

"Put your trust in God, my boys, but mind to keep your powder dry." Oliver Cromwell said that at the Battle of Edgehill in 1642, and I'm going to say something similar to you now. You have developed a financial divorce limbo plan—so fancy! You have completed your limbo budgets. You have figured out how you will cover your spending. Love it. Just one more thing you need: a disaster-recovery plan in case of emergencies. To paraphrase Mr. Cromwell for this situation: "Put your trust in your limbo plan, but mind to keep some cash in a sock in case things go to shit." Divorce limbo disasters include your ex quitting their job, draining the joint account, and leaving town. Wait! What about the interim support? How am I supposed to pay for the kids' sports? This is when you'll need that sock full of cash.

I want to be realistic. It's tough to prioritize a disaster-recovery plan. Not many people have go-bags packed and ready in their garage and a crossbow locked and loaded just in case (but they should!). Never fear, you don't need to take it that far. The key to your disaster-recovery plan is simply this: adaptability.

If divorce limbo disaster strikes, you'll need to adapt. You'll need to rethink your limbo plan. Maybe cut your spending, or reconsider your living arrangements, or ask your family for another loan. Disaster recovery is a team effort.

And with that, you've created financial security for your divorce limbo. This is a huge step, so reward yourself by taking a break or indulging in some self-care—because you're about to do the heavier lifting of preparing for your final settlement. I absolutely, positively know you can handle it. But odds are it's not going to be fun. We'll shoot for understandable and efficient. But fun isn't in the cards.

Back straight, shoulders back, chin up. We're goin' in.

A Quick Summary

- Divorcing can take time, so you need a divorce limbo financial plan for your security.

- Establish ground rules for joint financial decision-making.

- Prepare a personal and joint divorce limbo spending budget.

- Cover your spending with income, assets, or debt as appropriate.

- Plan for potential disaster and be ready to adapt.

6

Your Financial Homework

Arm yourself with the information you need to make your divorce deal.

LOOK! YOU'RE HALFWAY there! Wahoo!

Time to get to work on your financial homework in preparation for your final settlement. Once you've completed this homework, you'll understand where you are, financially, and where you'd like to go.

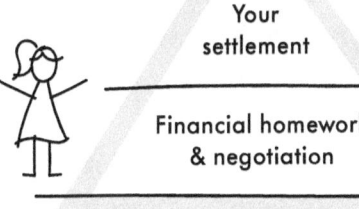

Your settlement

Financial homework & negotiation

Limbo plan: your secure foundation

Healthy thinking & good behavior

Information Gathering

Your first assignment is gathering and sharing information. If you're thinking this will be an easy part of your homework, like when your seventh grade geography teacher assigned map coloring, unfortunately it is not. The strange reality is that exchanging the necessary information to begin the process of dividing up your stuff and resolving the question of support is often one of the hardest parts of the whole divorce business.

But you need to understand your ex's financial circumstances, and they need to understand yours.

Hopefully, your ex wants to move through the process efficiently and will provide information without much fuss. But even if there is a whole bunch of fuss, you absolutely need financial disclosure to make decisions about your split. You may say that you aren't going to pursue your right to some of the assets initially. But you might change your mind when you discover that those assets are worth millions and were earned by borrowing against your family home.

Before you get started, I want to mention four things about this assignment to prepare you for the work to come.

Deep Breath #1: Disclosure is legally required

The exchange of information often provokes kicking and screaming. My belief is that people resist it for two reasons. One: it is a total pain to hunt down all the necessary information. Two: people think that sharing information will put them at a disadvantage.

I get the "total pain" reason. It's true. But it's either painful now or painful later. Actually, it's more like some pain now or way more pain later. Procrastinating prolongs the divorce business. And a prolonged divorce drives everyone insane and costs more money as your team spends their time (and your money!) fighting for access to information or defending you for denying access to information.

As for the "disadvantage" reason: I just have to say no. You do not have a choice about disclosing information. It is a legal requirement when you are getting divorced. Sure, some of the information might put you at a disadvantage. But that doesn't change the fact that you are obligated to disclose it, so you might as well get on with it.

Sharing information is required to get a deal done. Nobody, or nobody who is being well advised, can make decisions or reach a settlement without the facts.

Deep Breath #2: Enough is enough

You have to gather sufficient information, but you also have to be discerning. You may be tempted to dig through every detail, every shred of financial information, right down to your ex's dry-cleaning bills. However, there is a financial and emotional cost associated with gathering, analyzing, and discussing every detail and, often, it isn't worth it.

As you review the information, ask yourself: "What is the point of looking at this?" Maybe you'll have a good answer, like it tells you what your investments are worth. Or maybe the answer is just that it tells you how much your ex spent on a birthday gift for the new love interest and it's ten times what they used to spend on you. That last answer is a clue that you are off track and that there is no benefit to digging into that level of detail. In fact, there is a cost to your mental health. The key to this process is striking the right balance between what matters to your settlement and what does not.

Although I am not a big fan of making decisions without all of the important information, there is definitely such a thing as too much gathering and analyzing.

Try to avoid burying yourself in detail: do not dig up the bill for the cufflinks you bought for your ex on your first anniversary. That's just a waste of your time. But don't miss out on the information you need to make one of the most important decisions in your life either.

Buried in details up to your eyeballs

Missing loads of important information

Instead, shoot for the sweet spot between feeling buried by a ton of details and having insufficient information to make decisions. When in doubt, rely on your team to point you in the right direction with respect to the level of detail that will be required. Not having every detail is just fine, because you don't want to take so much time gathering information that you die before you get your deal done.

Deep Breath #3: All you can do is your best

Don't worry if you aren't sure what documents you need, or if you can't find certain information, or if your ex has the files. This is that "A for effort" type of homework. Gather what you can. And regroup with your team to develop a plan for filling in the gaps.

Deep Breath #4: Timing matters

Typically, you'll be looking for the most recent documents available. However, in some circumstances, you may need evidence of values at different times. Make sure you get guidance from your lawyer with respect to the relevant dates so you don't need to dig through your files more than once.

The Paper Mountain

Okey dokey, now it's time to gather some information. The complexity of your finances will determine the size of the piles you need to make. I've seen some pretty big piles over the years, but the size doesn't matter. The approach remains the same.

Pile #1: Assets (a.k.a. the good stuff)

The first step is to list all of your assets. At this point, don't worry about who owns what, just work to create a complete list of all the assets: yours, your ex's, and shared. This will include common stuff like real estate, companies, investments, retirement savings and pension plans, bank accounts, jewelry, and cars, as well as less common stuff like art, expensive stamp or wine collections, club memberships, and travel rewards. Just remember to not get carried away. You probably don't need to list your dishes, furniture, clothes, or the fishing gear. Just list the important stuff, the big-ish stuff. Now, if you have valuable antique furniture or the fishing gear fills up the entire basement, perhaps they will make the list. But since you don't want to be working on your divorce for the next ten years, avoid the insignificant items.

Next, for each item on your list, track down the best available documents that provide evidence about value and ownership: property tax assessments, company financial statements, investment statements, pension plan statements, bank statements, insurance appraisals for jewelry, and purchase or insurance documents for cars.

Again, I'm going to say that this is an "A for effort" situation. Do not try for perfection. You might not have relevant information for every asset. Heck, you might not have any information for some things. That's OK. You can work to fill in the blanks as you move through the process.

Pile #2: Debts (a.k.a. the bad stuff)

You guessed it. The next step is to list all of your debts: yours, your ex's, and shared. This will include common stuff like mortgages, lines of credit, credit card debt, car loans, and leases. And less common stuff like personal loans from family and friends and the final remaining payment on your golf club membership.

For each debt, track down supporting documents: bank statements, credit card statements, loan and lease agreements, that napkin showing you owe your mom $10,000. Broken record time: A for effort.

Pile #3: Income

When it comes to income, you'll typically want to gather the last few years of information about your earnings. Three years is probably plenty, but every situation is unique, so you might need to go back a bit further. Your tax returns are an excellent source of information and might be all you need. But if your finances are complicated by earnings within companies or partnerships or trusts, you will need the statements for those entities too. Again, the tax returns for those entities would be an excellent source of information about earnings.

Pile #4: Expenses

If you've completed your limbo plan, you've already done much of this homework. If you haven't gotten there yet, now is the time to gather information regarding your spending. Annual or monthly spending summaries from credit card and bank statements can be super useful. If those aren't available, gather monthly statements from your commonly used credit cards and bank accounts. Your accountant can help you summarize that information. For the purposes of planning for divorce limbo, your settlement, and beyond, the budgeting process we discussed on pages 136–141 will be super useful. If you procrastinated back in chapter 5, now would be a good time to get to work on that limbo budget.

Sorting the Piles

You're off to a great start. You've gathered all the information that you can. Now what?

Your next step is to categorize the first two piles—all of the assets and debts—into three pie pieces: yours, your ex's, and shared. The "yours" slice is your excluded property, the stuff you don't need to share with your ex, and the "your ex's" slice is their excluded property, the stuff they don't need to share with you. And the shared stuff... well, that's the stuff you need to share.

Even though that sounds simple, this is another one of those times when the devil can be hiding in the details. You'll need the help of your lawyer to get this right. The question of what stuff should be shared is often subject to some debate. Maybe your situation is simple: you've been married forever, started out with no assets, and the law in your area says you share everything fifty-fifty. Your list will be pretty darn easy because every last thing will go in the "shared stuff" column. But maybe it's more complicated than that. Perhaps you haven't been married long, you both brought assets with you into the marriage, or you inherited some cash from your grandma's estate and the law in your area says some of those pre-existing or inherited assets should be excluded property.

This is one of those times when you don't know what you don't know, so I recommend that you get help.

Here is an example of a categorized list of assets and debts. In this example, your inheritance from your grandma is considered excluded property—it's yours. And your ex's cash gift from their dad is also excluded property—it's theirs. The rest of the stuff is shared. It's common for the "shared" list to be the longest.

	Your stuff	Your Ex's stuff	Shared stuff
Assets			
Cottage from Grandma	$ 175,000		
Inherited jewelry	10,000		
Gift $$ from Dad		$ 80,000	
Family home			$ 250,000
Family business			150,000
Cars			50,000
Pension			300,000
Investments			450,000
Debts			
Mortgage			(100,000)
Line of credit			(50,000)
Credit card debt			(25,000)
Net worth	**$ 185,000**	**$ 80,000**	**$ 1,025,000**

Dividing the Shared Stuff

You've come a long way. You now have a clear picture of where you are, financially speaking. It's time to begin figuring out where you want to go. To me, that's more fun. But I'm an accountant so I know my version of fun is a little twisted. Still, I'd like you to view this next part with some optimism because you are putting your mind to your future instead of your past. And while I know that all this number-crunching sort of sucks, I encourage you to view it as the first step in creating your big, fat fabulous future.

With that optimistic mindset, it's time to consider how you want to divide the shared stuff. This is the stuff that should be divided equally, fifty-fifty. But that's easier said than done. Lots of stuff doesn't actually divide. You can't cut the family home in half. Your cars probably won't run if you slice them down the center. How do you handle it if you both want the same stuff? And if one of you wants to keep something, then you aren't selling it on the open market. So how do you decide what it's worth? This is complicated!

Don't panic. To quote Marie Forleo, "everything is figureoutable." (Also the title of one of her books, and a belief that will serve you well throughout your divorce.) By the end of your homework assignment, as you head into your negotiation, you'll have a plan for what stuff you want to keep and what stuff you are prepared to give up, sell, or share with your ex (heaven help us all, but we'll get to that later).

But in order to establish that plan, you need to know the value of all the stuff. You really can't decide what stuff you want to keep until you know what you will have to pay for it. Of course you want those Jimmy Choo shoes... until you find out they cost $1,500! And in divorce, when you decide to keep something from the shared pile, you essentially have to *buy* half of it from your ex.

This is often a mind-bender for people. "What are you talking about—I have to buy it? It's my stuff." When we are living in our homes, traveling to our cottages, or driving our cars, it doesn't cross our mind that we only own half of our stuff. But, actually, it's shared stuff. And if you want to keep it, you have to pay your ex for their half.

As we move along into figuring out what stuff is worth, I want you to keep these two concepts in mind:

1. You only own half of the stuff you want to keep. You need to pay your ex for their half.

2. Your ex only owns half of the stuff they want to keep. They need to pay you for your half.

And now, let's talk value.

Valuing the Shared Stuff

So, we've agreed: you won't make the final decisions about what you'd like to keep or give up until you have an idea of what the stuff is worth. Don't forget, you have to divide both the good stuff (the assets) and the not-so-good stuff (the debts). Time to talk about when and how to value the stuff.

If you intend to sell some of the shared stuff, then you don't need to worry about figuring out what it's worth. You'll just sell it and split the sale proceeds. Easy-peasy.

If you intend to continue to share some of the shared stuff, then you don't need to worry about figuring out what it's worth. I'll call that "somewhat easy" because continuing to share stuff with your ex isn't easy. Remember my sermon on cohabitation during divorce? I don't like to be bossy (I can hear my husband laughing), but think long and hard before you plan on sharing stuff with your ex. But, while sharing stuff is likely to be challenging, at least you don't need to worry about valuing what's shared. So, easy-ish-peasy-ish.

Now, the stuff you or your ex want to keep is a more challenging category. This is stuff you aren't going to sell to a stranger or continue to share. And that means this is stuff you need to value, as in, figure out what the heck it's worth. Some of the stuff will be easy to value, and some of the stuff will be hard to value.

You could hire experts to value every last thing, but that would probably be overkill. Or, you could try to value everything yourselves, but that would probably be underkill (not officially a word, but it's my book). The key here is striking a reasonable balance. Remember the girl on the wrecking ball from page 154? Same idea.

Here are two things to keep in mind.

Price Point #1: Size matters

If something is small relative to your wealth, it might not make sense to have it professionally appraised. Yes, I just suggested you decide whether to hire a professional to assess value based on the value of the stuff. How the heck do you know the value? You haven't hired a professional yet! I get that this is a bit cart-before-the-horse-ish. But you can probably make a reasonable guess at whether or not something is too insignificant to worry about.

For example, maybe your ex has an antique car. Not one of those awesome restored antique cars. Just an old beater that they swore year after year they were going to fix up while it rotted away in the garage. Let's say you're pretty well-to-do and you wouldn't blink if a meteor fell on that car and crushed it into a fine dust. Probably doesn't make sense to have it appraised. A ballpark value will do. Or maybe your ex has one of those awesome restored antique cars. The kind that is worth big bucks. Probably makes sense to have it appraised.

If the ballpark value of something is really small relative to your net worth, just estimate the value and move on. No additional work required.

Price Point #2: Complex stuff requires expert valuation

Moving on to stuff that isn't really small...

For some of your stuff, value is going to be obvious: your bank accounts, including checking and savings accounts, and your loan and credit card balances. You'll just need the most recent statements and you can cross those off your to-do list.

For other stuff, values won't be obvious: real estate, your ex's specialty stamp collection, your flower shop. For this kind of complex stuff, you're going to need some help determining values. And that's where the experts come in.

Here are my three recommendations for working with expert valuators:

Consider using a joint expert. I mean, find someone that both you and your ex can agree on to perform the necessary appraisals and valuations. Because if you hire your own expert, then your ex will probably hire a different expert. And you might even need to hire a third tie-breaker expert. All those experts means a smaller pie left for you and your ex to divide, and so sharing the experts will save you time and money. If you're worried that the shared expert will like your ex more than you and modify their conclusions to benefit your ex (yikes! scary!), trust me when I say that is very unlikely. I assure you, the expert almost certainly likes themself more than they like you or your ex, and their professional reputation depends on them being impartial. They won't compromise their own livelihood to benefit either of you.

Remember that the expert's opinion isn't gospel. The expert's opinion about the value of your stuff is important, but it doesn't mean that you or your ex has no choice but to live with that recommended value. If one expert's opinion seems completely out-to-lunch to you, consider getting a second opinion. Or, consider the possibility that it's *you* who may be off base. When it comes to our stuff, we tend to get attached, and personal attachment can lead to valuing stuff inaccurately.

Make sure the valuation is timely. Consider the timing of any expert's opinion about values. The divorce process can take an insanely long time, and expert reports may be out of date by the time the deal is done. If loads of time has passed since you had your stuff valued, consider getting the opinion updated. Of course, you'll want to consider *how* the conclusions might have changed and whether or not that change would be to your advantage. Maybe your ex will be buying you out of the family business. If the company's earnings increased 30 percent since the valuation, then it might be worth investing in an updated opinion. But if sales have plummeted, maybe an updated valuation isn't in your best interest.

Analyzing Your Stuff

When you know what things are worth, you'll be ready to decide what you want to sell, share, keep, and give up. Simple to say and often difficult to do.

Do you want it or not? You'd think this would be an easy question to answer, but proceed with caution because your brain is under the influence of divorce. This might mean you don't exactly know what you want, or it might mean that what you want is changing. Some soul searching may be required to work through the "do I want it?" question. Don't rush, and understand that you are making a preliminary plan. Divorce business takes time, so you'll probably have the opportunity to change your mind.

This is not a purely pragmatic exercise with the goal of maximizing your value. I'm an accountant not a robot, dammit. But the more pragmatic you can be, the more likely it is that you'll maximize your value.

When you're pragmatic, you don't keep the family home when your ex insists you must buy them out at a big, fat premium. When you're pragmatic, you agree to sell that painting to the blue-haired rich lady who offers twice its value because it reminds her of her childhood. I'm not saying that pragmatism is better than romanticism. I'm saying that romanticism comes at a price and I want you to examine whether or not you can afford it. You totally might be able to afford it. Make sure you can by crunching the numbers. Deal?

Here is proof that pragmatism should come before romanticism. I made this up without any sort of scientific study, but I still think it's right:

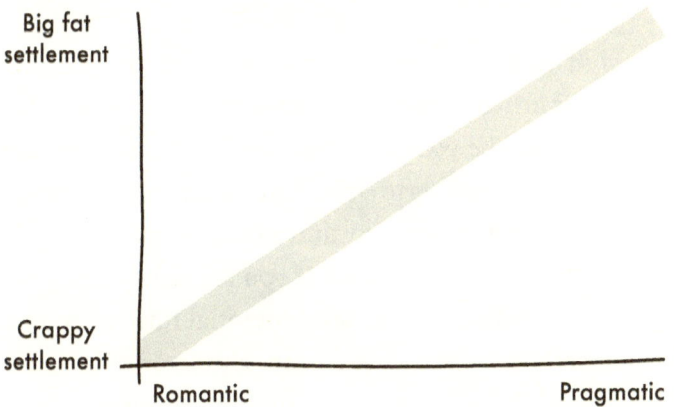

Time to be Pollypragmatist and not Pollyanna.

Here are the things you need to consider when deciding between sell, share, keep, or give-it-up (a.k.a. sell it to your ex). Forgive me; there's lots for you to think about here, but this is a big deal—maybe the biggest financial deal of your life—so you want to think carefully.

Pile #1: The sell pile

Again, we're starting easy. Basically, this is a pile of leftovers. You don't want it. Your ex doesn't want it. And you don't want to share it. My favorite pile.

Pile #2: The share pile

I view continuing to share stuff as an occasionally necessary evil. It's not my first choice for you. I actually kinda hate it. But there are a couple of circumstances in which it might make sense.

The stuff is next to impossible to value. Maybe you have some artwork from an undervalued artist now on his deathbed. Maybe you own some stock in a small private company that is hoping to strike it rich with a breakthrough technology, potentially worth nothing or millions. It is dang hard to value that stuff. If you are risk-averse, perhaps you're willing to give up a potential future windfall for a small pile of real-world cash. However, think hard about how you'll feel if your ex sells that painting or those penny stocks for millions two years after your split. Consider putting that sort of stuff in the share pile until the timing makes sense to sell and split the cash.

The stuff is too valuable. Maybe you own stuff that neither you nor your ex can afford to keep on your own. Neither of you can afford to buy the other's half. Maybe it doesn't make sense to sell the stuff, such as the cabin that you want to leave to your kids when you die or the family business that's growing like crazy. You might want to consider a longer-term sharing arrangement for that sort of stuff. Mamma mia. I can't believe I'm suggesting that. Be warned that this is a mother lode of joint decision-making challenges. Even if you and your ex are happy sharing-unicorns, your next mates might not be as well adjusted. Still, it could be a necessary evil.

Piles #3 and #4: The "keep it" and "give it up" piles

Some things are divisible: the bank account, the cash in your mattress, certain investments. That makes it simple. You'll just divide those down the middle.

But lots of stuff isn't divisible: real estate, cars, artwork. And that's where things get trickier. If you aren't selling it or sharing it, then either you'll keep it or your ex will keep it.

Obviously there will be non-financial considerations in your decision-making process. Even we accountants understand that decisions on what to keep and what to give up aren't strictly pragmatic and financial. Just remember the pragmatism-romanticism chart! But even being purely pragmatic, there are still complicated considerations.

Here are five points to consider when working through the keep-give decisions:

What to do with home sweet home. Your toughest decision regarding shared stuff may relate to your family home or recreation property, so please proceed cautiously. When I separated, I attached being a good mom to keeping my house. I told a friend that I would move heaven and earth to hang on to it. My friend's response to my dramatic statement was, "Why?" In struggling to answer, I realized that I was putting too much weight on the importance of the house. Dang, that was powerful and freeing, and it helped me recalibrate. Now, I'm not suggesting you give up the family home or cottage, just that you consider your decision in light of your financial situation rather than under the pressure of any emotional reactions. That said, if you are genuinely emotionally attached to something and can afford to pay for it, then proceed, if with caution. Remember that you are vulnerable to overpaying or over-sacrificing in other areas when pushing to retain stuff to which you attribute non-financial value.

Mind the market timing. Typically, the value of stuff fluctuates over time. All things being equal, you'd rather keep stuff that has a low value, since you'll be buying half of it from your ex, and give up stuff that has a high value, since they'll be buying half of it from you.

Buy low, sell high. Another rule that sounds so easy but is actually pretty tough. Since you don't have a crystal ball, it's hard to know where values are heading. Get the help of your accountant to make a judgment call regarding future values.

Consider volatility. When choosing what to keep and what to give up, you need to understand volatility. An accountant is useful here, too, to help you understand the volatility of the value your assets. Basically, the value of different stuff fluctuates in different ways. The value of some stuff fluctuates like this:

That sort of stuff gets my accountant-heart pounding, and not in a good way. The value of other stuff fluctuates like this:

I'm not saying that one is necessarily better than the other (unless you are an accountant, and then clearly the second one is better). But if you hate the idea of overpaying more than you love the idea of underpaying, you might want to stick with the stuff with less volatility. We'll call you risk-averse and you can sit by me. On the other hand, if you love the idea of underpaying and can live with the idea of overpaying, you might be open to keeping the stuff with more volatility. We'll call you a risk-taker. Actually, you can sit by me too. You keep things interesting.

Consider liquidity. Access to cold hard cash is right up there with lists and goals in my accountant-heart. Liquidity is important to your financial security and success. Liquidity means you can jump on that deal when you see it or do without income while you travel through Asia. Overall wealth is key to your long-term financial success, but if you don't have some liquidity and you can't pay your phone bill next month, that wealth isn't a big help. If you're wondering about your level of liquidity, imagine this: You've been charged with a crime you didn't commit and need to skip town. You need cash, so you drain your accounts, max out your credit, and beg friends and family for some dough. If you don't have enough to pay for groceries for a week, you probably don't have enough liquidity. As your accountant, I'd like you to shoot for enough liquidity to be able to cover your costs for a minimum of six months. Your mom would likely agree.

Remember the tax implications. You're probably groaning inside and wanting to put down this book and pour yourself a cold drink. But don't worry, I'll keep it short and sweet. Taxes can be a big, big number. Sometimes, you can transfer your stuff between you and your ex without paying any tax now. Sometimes, you can't. Sometimes, after you've divided up all your stuff and you eventually sell some of that stuff, you'll have to pay tax. Sometimes, you don't. (Ha! Now you really want that cold drink!) The point is to not forget about taxes as you split your stuff, and to do what you can to avoid a tax bill, or at least an immediate tax bill. Your goal should be to defer, defer, defer. All things being equal, you would rather pay your tax later than sooner. Although lots of people don't like the idea of a big future tax bill, it makes way more financial sense than a big present tax bill. Don't worry—you don't need to be a tax expert yourself. Just make sure your accountant is on it.

Decision-Making

Now you know what you have, you know what it's worth, and you understand the key elements to consider when choosing what to sell, share, keep, and give up. Now it's time to split up the pie. Really, you've done the hard stuff. This part will be like that map-coloring you were hoping for.

The first step is to categorize your stuff into two lists: one list of stuff that you'll be sharing with your ex or selling to split the proceeds, and another list of stuff that you want to keep or give up to your ex. Keep in mind that these lists will evolve, and that you'll want to be flexible during the negotiation so you can gain advantages. But it's good to have a clear starting point in mind as you head into your negotiation.

Here's an example of List #1:

	Share	Sell
Family business	$ 150,000	
Family home		$ 250,000
Mortgage		(100,000)
Total	**$ 150,000**	**$ 150,000**

Um, that's a pretty short list. But, in real life, people don't often end up sharing and selling much stuff. So art is imitating life. You've decided to share the family business (heaven help you). You made this choice because the business is growing like crazy, you run it together, and you believe it makes sense to sell to a stranger in a few years. And you've decided, somewhat sadly, to sell the family home, pay off the mortgage, and split the remaining sale proceeds.

Here's an example of List #2:

	Keep	Give up
Cars	$ 25,000	$ 25,000
Pension		300,000
Investments	450,000	
Line of credit	(50,000)	
Credit card debt	(25,000)	
Total	$ 400,000	$ 325,000

Wait a sec. Now you have more than your ex. But this is the fifty-fifty pile so that doesn't work. Again, this is usually the way it goes in real life. It's very rare that things end up exactly equal after you sort your stuff into piles. In this case, that means you need to make an equalization payment to your ex.

In our example, you have $75,000 more than they have. In order to equalize your assets, you'll need to pay them $37,500. What? Why not $75,000?

In the world of dividing stuff up when you get divorced, you've got to get used to thinking in halves. In the situation in List #2, if you pay your ex $37,500, then you are left with $362,500. That's $400,000, less the payment of $37,500. And your ex now has the same amount: $362,500. That's $325,000 plus the payment of $37,500. Make sense? Honestly, I still have to remind myself of this "thinking in halves" rule, and I do this for a living. So don't worry if this is a bit of a mind-bender.

The Postdivorce Budget

And with that, you've finished your preliminary planning with respect to the division of assets. A huge accomplishment. Happy dances and high fives all 'round! And more good news: you're very close to wrapping up your homework.

Now comes your last assignment: putting your mind to your postdivorce budget. Can you believe it? We're talking about life after your divorce! I hope this good news eases the pain of knowing that you're headed for some more number crunching.

You might be thinking, "Postdivorce?! Who the heck cares about postdivorce, I can barely handle duringdivorce!" But hear me out. You need to consider your postdivorce finances to make sure that your plan actually works.

The fact that you have a preliminary plan is amazing, spectacular, fantastic! Lots of people don't get this far. But if your initial plan isn't viable, you have to make some changes, and it's better to know that sooner rather than later. Now is the time to recalibrate, if necessary.

Frankly, your lifestyle will change as a result of your divorce. In some ways it will be better, but you will not maintain the lifestyle "to which you have become accustomed" because that lifestyle was built around a relationship that is over.

For most people, dividing assets in half and establishing two households means there will be less income available to support spending. You may rethink keeping the luxurious family home if it means that you have to postpone your retirement until age eighty-five. So let's get to it.

Step #1: Determine your postdivorce spending

First, brush off that spending budget you made for your limbo plan and update it for your vision of your postdivorce life. Now, I understand that making long-term plans at a time when your life is turned upside down is difficult. Keep in mind that while today you might want to take a vow of poverty and live off-grid in a hut in the jungle, that desire will most likely pass as you settle into your new life. Just do your best to envision your postdivorce lifestyle because your plans will likely evolve as you move through the cycles of grief, loss, relief, anger, or happiness of your divorce.

Step #2: Estimate your earnings

Next, you'll need to estimate your income. Maybe you're working and you'll have earnings. Maybe you run your own business, which is generating a profit. And maybe your asset division will result in investments that will kick off income.

Step #3: Figure out support entitlement

And now back to the elephant in the room: support. This is often one of the most challenging issues to resolve during divorce. There are lots of variables to consider when determining support, so this is definitely not a do-it-yourself issue. For planning purposes, include a support number on the conservative end of the range of possible outcomes. If you'll be paying support, round up. If you'll be receiving support, round down. Of course you will push for the best result, but you don't want to bank on it.

Figuring out your support entitlement or obligation can be tough. Living with the ongoing management of the arrangement can make splitting up your stuff look like tea and cookies at grandma's house.

When you are the one obligated to pay, you may be tempted to blame your ex for draining your bank account and being the reason that you aren't spending winters on a beach. When you are the one entitled to receive, you may spend your nights wondering how the hell your ex just bought a luxury car when they reported earnings of $7,500 last year.

The best approach to the issue of support? Keep it simple. Avoid convoluted formulas or arrangements that require a bunch of ongoing, detailed analysis.

Step #4: Balance your income and your spending

Once you have your best estimates of your spending, income, and support, it's time to see whether or not your income covers your spending.

If the answer is yes, fabulous! You are ready to move into your negotiation.

But if the answer is no, you need to rethink your plan—because it won't work if your income doesn't cover your spending. Maybe this means selling the family cottage, renting out the basement suite in your home, traveling less, or working more. Be open minded. The cottage won't be very relaxing if you are fielding collection calls instead of lounging on the dock. I promise, you can still create a fabulous life without the cottage, and then you'll have a plan that works.

PAUSE AND celebrate this big accomplishment. You have your plan to begin negotiating your final settlement. Since the divorce process is a long haul, please celebrate wins as you go. It will improve your stamina.

A final word about your plan: remain adaptable. You've got a plan and that's awesome. But divorce is a process, and it takes two. You'll benefit more and suffer less if you remain flexible.

In the next chapter, we'll brush up on your negotiating skills so you can turn your plan into reality.

A Quick Summary

- Gather information about assets, debts, income, and expenses.

- Categorize your stuff between yours, your ex's, and shared.

- Figure out what the shared stuff is worth.

- Decide how you'd like to deal with the shared stuff: sell it, share it, keep it, or give it up.

- Prepare a postdivorce budget in order to make sure your financial plan works.

7

Negotiating 101

The business of divorce is a negotiation, not a battle.

DURING DIVORCE, you aren't functioning at your best. In the middle of the heartache, the upheaval, and radical life changes, you need to negotiate the division of assets and income with your ex. This is a daunting challenge and also a strange shift. You were married, teammates, but now you and your ex are sitting across the table in a negotiation as adversaries. I say negotiation because that's how I want you to view the business of your divorce. Not as a battle but as a negotiation. And while negotiations often include some win-lose scenarios, they often result in fewer combined losses than the alternative of litigation. Litigation is uncertain and expensive.

So far, I've managed to convince all of my clients that negotiation is a better way to start than litigation. However, I have seen some friends dive headlong into litigation in the heat of the early days of their separation, and it hasn't been pretty. Years of conflict and lots of suffering were the result. Obviously I'm comparing apples and oranges, because every relationship and every divorce is unique. But I've had an up-close view of many divorces, and a theme has emerged. Negotiating during divorce is tough but litigating is tougher.

Granted, if your ex won't deal fairly in an honest attempt to reach an agreement, you'll likely be heading to court. And even if both you and your ex are trying to deal fairly, you might not succeed in getting a deal done. But it's worth the effort, so give negotiation a solid shot. Good news! Statistics are on your side. Most people negotiate and settle. Most people are able to avoid divorce court. So, let's prepare you to be a spectacular negotiator.

Before we talk details, remember that negotiating is an art. There is no one right way or best way to do it. But there are some concepts or guidelines that can serve you, regardless of the path your divorce negotiations travel.

It's Only Money

I recommend that you start chanting this mantra whenever you get the chance. Don't get me wrong. You need money. It provides vital things like food and shelter. I have built a career helping people like you manage your finances because I know that money is super-duper important. But it's only money. A tool for buying stuff you need and want. Nothing more. Nothing less. Avoid wrapping it up with more meaning or importance.

How do you do that? By remembering the following two principles.

Principle #1: Money doesn't represent your worth

I live in an affluent community filled with people ranging from well-off to insanely loaded. As a member of the community, location on the financial continuum is part of your identity. It isn't necessarily obvious where you land on that continuum, but there are clues. Do you have the latest "it" bag? Is your house the size of a boutique hotel? Do you have a fancy car, or ten? You get the idea.

When my husband and I began struggling in our marriage, we engaged in a lot of retail therapy. We bought fancy watches, diamonds, cars, whether we could afford them or not. And as I accumulated some pretty things, my ego got attached to that level of consumption. That phase wrapped up when we faced the fact that our relationship was in serious trouble. Retail therapy ended and actual therapy began.

We sold our fancy-for-us house and bought a smaller place in a less desirable part of our still wonderfully desirable town. When I was talking about the move with a lovely acquaintance and fellow member of the local tennis club, I explained that we were moving to get out from under a big mortgage that was partially responsible for creating strain in our marriage. I immediately saw her shoulders sag and she quietly told me that they also felt the stress of a big mortgage.

Acknowledging my financial reality led to a stronger connection between me and that lovely lady. The fabulous silver lining of embracing the shift in your financial identity is an opportunity to find something more important to drive your connections with other people. I don't mean to suggest there is a problem with having lots of dough, or nice cars, or fancy handbags. The problems arise when we build our self-worth on the foundation of said dough.

Remember, it's only money.

Principle #2: Money isn't a tool for vengeance, control, or continued connection with your ex

Standard scenario: Your marriage is on the rocks. The relationship sucks up more time and energy than it did when it wasn't on the rocks. Your heart starts pounding when you hear them come in the front door. Not the heart pounding you had when you were newlyweds but still pounding. At this point, you are focusing a ton of energy on your relationship. And it's in that highly focused state that you begin the business of your divorce.

You go from having many points of connection with your ex to having a few: What are we going to do about the money? And what are we going to do about the kids? You work hard to do right and protect your kids; or maybe you have no kids, which means you pour all the unfinished business of your marriage into the other remaining point of connection: money. That's how money becomes way more than money.

That's the standard scenario, but you're not going to duplicate it, right? What you need to do is redirect your energy elsewhere so that the money issue doesn't become a way to control or continue the relationship, or a tool for vengeance.

Let's think of a better scenario: Your marriage is on the rocks. The relationship sucks up more time and energy than it did when it wasn't on the rocks. Your heart starts pounding when you hear them come in the front door. You realize you better find an outlet for all that energy or you'll bring it into the business of your divorce. You take up kickboxing, or rock climbing, or ultra-running. You work through your rage or grief or loneliness with your counselor and not with your ex. And when it comes to the negotiation of your financial split, you remember that it's only money.

Control Your Fear

Divorce leads to fear, about lots of scary stuff. The fearful thoughts that you might attach to your divorce negotiation often go something like this: "I'm going to run out of money. I'll have to get a crappy job to pay for groceries." Or, "I'm being cheated. My ex is hiding assets from me and lying about their income."

Your fears are relevant and you should pay attention to them. However, there is a risk of overemphasizing the importance or relevance of your fears. Consider taking them with a grain of salt, because they shouldn't become the primary factor in your decision-making.

When I'm working to put my fear in its place it helps me to see that my fear is not *me*. I am just the one observing it, experiencing it. To do this, I created an imaginary person I call my fear freak. She wears her hair in a bun, flosses after every meal, makes lists for everything, hates spicy foods, and is always worried about me. I take her ideas with a grain of salt. Maybe this same strategy will work for you. But if not, I encourage you to find your own way to loosen fear's grip even though it's unlikely that you'll be able to eliminate the fear altogether.

You are not alone if you didn't have a crystal-clear picture of your family finances heading into your divorce. During the process you will get the facts, and that means no more blissful ignorance. It's common to make some surprising discoveries. Perhaps you hadn't realized the total amount of debt you were carrying. Perhaps you hadn't realized you have been spending more than you are earning. All of that newfound information might be scary. In any case, you now have to contemplate a dramatic change in your finances. And your fear freak is not going to like it.

Every divorce is unique, but, generally speaking, you'll be dividing up your assets, debts, income, and expenses, and your pie is going to feel smaller. When you're married, you share a pie with your spouse, and it's common to look at that entire pie and consider it yours. When you get divorced, usually you are cutting that pie in half and going your separate ways. That's likely going to feel like a financial kick in the gut.

Maybe you've liked the idea of "being kept in the manner to which you have become accustomed." I get that desire, but hanging on to that thought is not helpful. Your financial life is going to change because you will be dividing up your assets, losing the economies that come with sharing a household, paying your divorce team, and perhaps suffering from the lower productivity and income that often comes with divorce.

Unfortunately, getting divorced can take a ridiculously long time, so you'll have lots of time to anticipate your financial postdivorce future. It's all right to feel scared but don't allow your fear freak to lead you down a rabbit hole. Don't let her lead you to spend years and thousands of dollars on forensic audits. Don't let her lead you to freeze, avoid decisions, and so forgo a negotiated settlement in return for a court-imposed arrangement. Maybe a forensic audit is completely necessary because your ex is lying and cheating. Maybe a negotiated settlement is unattainable because your ex refuses to budge on even the smallest issue. Maybe your worst fears turn into realities. However, if you allow your fear about those possibilities to dominate your mental landscape, you will certainly create more problems, more suffering.

Don't let your fear freak turn into your primary decision-maker.

Now let's dig into some specific negotiating tips.

Pro-Negotiator Tip #1: Mind your emotional temperature

Divorce negotiations run a high risk of turning sour. Once, you loved each other, but now you're more likely to hate each other than to feel indifference. You might experience strong emotions in response to the behavior of your ex and those emotions can derail your negotiation. I'm not saying you need to be an ice queen, but it might not hurt in this situation.

**Pro-Negotiator Tip #2:
Strengthen your boundaries**

You know that moment when you're barely holding yourself together (and I know you do because you're going through a divorce) and then someone gives you a hug and you burst into tears? The hug reduces your boundaries to the point where you can't control your emotions anymore.

We have unique boundaries for every person and situation in our life. Boundaries are neither good nor bad, but we get into trouble when the thickness of one of our boundaries is a mismatch for the person or situation. Here are boundaries that are a good fit:

Boundary with the grocery clerk | Boundary with your friend from work | Boundary with your best friend

This means: When the grocery clerk asks you how you are, you answer, "I'm fine, thanks. How are you?"

When your work colleague asks you how you are, you answer, "Oh, I've seen better days but I'm hanging in there. Thanks for asking."

And when your best friend asks you how you are, you answer, "I'm terrible and I desperately need a hug."

Setting boundaries is not a question of honesty or authenticity. It's just that things get weird if you start telling the grocery clerk that you need a hug. To successfully navigate your negotiation, your boundaries with your ex have to change from this:

To this:

See? Your boundaries need to be way thicker than the ones you have even with the grocery clerk. That way, when your ex insists that you return your wedding ring, that demand will bounce off you. I'm not saying you'll hand over the wedding ring because you don't care anymore, but when your boundaries are thick you will be able to calmly tell them to stuff it with a smile on your face. No, I'm kidding. You'll be able to decide, with the advice of your amazing team, to tell them to stuff it or to hand over the ring for the right price, whatever makes the most sense for you in the negotiation. When you are wrapped up in good boundaries, your emotional temperature drops by a few degrees.

Pro-Negotiator Tip #3: Avoid making stuff up

When you were together you had a lot of information about your ex, maybe more than you ever wanted to know. Then you separate, and that flow of information is reduced. For some couples, that flow goes into a slow decline. For others, the steel walls of privacy slam down.

Either way, you likely won't know as much about what your ex is thinking, or feeling, or doing as you did when you were together. Hello, vacuum. Resist the urge to fill that information vacuum by making stuff up.

When they demand that you hand over your wedding ring, you might make up a story that they never really loved you. OK, I have no idea whether your ex loved you. But I do know that the demand for the ring is a crappy indicator. Maybe they loved you so much they can't think straight. Maybe they want you to suffer like they're suffering. Since there's no way to know, just stick with the facts. They're demanding the ring. Plain and simple. What do you want to do about that?

Avoid making stuff up and your emotional temperature will drop by a few more degrees.

Pro-Negotiator Tip #4: Mind your speed

In divorce, you don't want to move too fast or too slow. When I began divorce work, I wanted to get deals done as fast as possible for my clients. But now I understand that people who are getting divorced often need time to work through their thoughts and feelings about the end of their relationship throughout the process.

Be sensitive to the idea that you might need that time. Be sensitive to the idea that your ex might need that time. Take time if you need it and have the patience to give time if your ex needs it. Avoid imposing unreasonable time pressure on yourself or them.

But, also, don't let the ball roll around on your side of the court, because unreasonable delays can derail the negotiation. Make decisions, instruct your team, keep moving. In the age of instant responses, divorce can be one of the few remaining processes that incorporate painfully slow exchanges of information and perspectives.

Beware of letter-exchanging campaigns between the lawyers that move at a snail's pace. Instead, maintain momentum with prompt disclosure of information, responses to inquiries, offers, and counteroffers. When the time is right, make reasonable movements in your position instead of remaining entrenched. Horse-trade. Brainstorm creative solutions. Keep things moving.

Pro-Negotiator Tip #5: Don't lie, cheat, or steal

I'm going to assume that you are a decent person. Since you're taking the time to read my book, I like you. Still, divorce can bring out the raging crazy person in all of us, and sometimes that raging crazy person might be tempted to think that the ends justify the means.

If your ex controlled your finances and had you on a strict allowance for your entire marriage, you may feel justified in siphoning cash into an offshore account before making your escape from the relationship.

If your ex didn't lift a finger during your marriage, stands to inherit millions of dollars, and is entitled to half of your hard-earned retirement savings, you may feel justified in telling them that the pension plan went belly up.

Don't.

Pragmatically speaking, if you get caught, your divorce will become infinitely messier and you will likely be headed to court for a resolution. Take it from me, judges usually don't approve of the "lying, cheating, stealing" approach—and your friends and family might not want to hang out with you anymore either.

There are payoffs to being an honest person: better sleep, better relationship, better odds that you'll have a productive negotiation that ends in a deal, and, if you end up in court, the judge viewing you as an honest person instead of a liar and a thief. Better, right?

Getting Comfortable with Concessions

Financial divorce deals have many issues. This isn't as simple as buying tomatoes at a farmers' market. You want to buy the tomatoes. The farmer wants to sell the tomatoes. The only issue to resolve is the price. Simple. But even in relatively simple divorces, there are usually a few complex issues. With the help of your team, you need to develop a plan to handle that complexity. One big element of that plan is figuring out when and where to make concessions.

A divorce deal isn't finalized until you've agreed on everything. This is important because it means that whatever path you take to reach the finish line, there is no deal until you arrive at that finish line. In other words, we are simply looking for the path that gets you to the best finish line. Don't let ego or emotions lead you off that path. If you're saying things like, "I am *not* blinking first. That jerk needs to pay for what they've done," or "I just gave up the wedding china. It's their turn to give something up.

I'm not budging," then you might be allowing your ego or emotions to determine your concession strategy. Although concessions might feel like a bitter pill, it's better to swallow that pill and keep your eye on the prize, the complete and final deal.

Pick the concession strategy that gets you to the best finish line. Don't focus on how you feel in the first 500 meters because what matters is the finish line. A deal is not a deal until it's a done deal.

Here are some things to consider when planning your concession strategy.

Deal Maker #1: Both of you must make concessions

First, do not expect your deal to look like this:

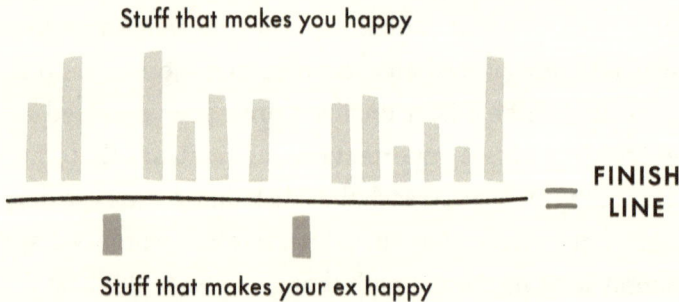

This is not how negotiations work. Your ex would be better off going to court.

And don't expect your deal to look like this, either:

Don't let that happen. You'd be better off going to court.

Deal Maker #2: An early concession approach can be effective

Consider making a concession first: giving something up, giving in, letting your ex win. Maybe give up something you know they really want and that you don't care so much about—the collection of fishing poles, the fishing boat, or the ice-fishing hut. An early concession can get things started on the right foot and shows your ex how it should be done. See? This is what we do. We give and take. I'll give first and now it's your turn.

An "early concession" negotiation might look like this:

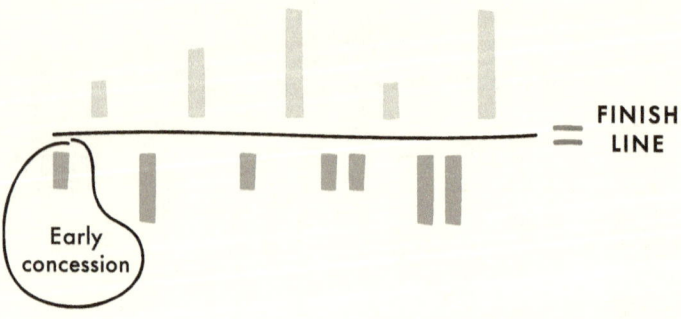

Your ex might not get this approach the first time, but stick with it. Consider front-loading a bunch of concessions until you get through to them. The "front-loaded concessions" negotiation might look like this:

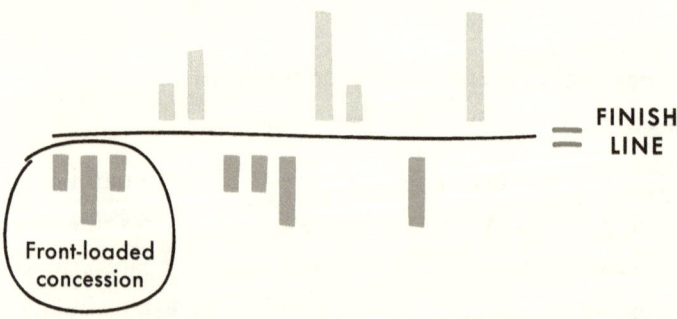

Notice the size and number of the bars. It's the *exact same deal*. It doesn't matter who gave up what or when. But, actually, it does. With the front-loaded concessions, your ex will get pretty attached to the deal. You're halfway through the negotiation and they're feeling pretty bloody good and maybe they finally start to see how it should be done. But even if they never see it, they're still attached to the deal and they may be more inclined to yield to your demands in the later stages.

Deal Maker #3: An early strength approach can be effective too

Now let's say your ex is a bully and thinks they should get everything they want and you should get zip. You might need to ditch the early concession approach in favor of an early strength approach.

Again, it's the same deal. You simply employed some early strength to shake your ex out of the notion that they will get everything they want.

Deal Maker #4: There's a time to dig in

OK, concessions are important, but please don't concede on issues that are vital for you. If you would rather gouge out your eyes than give up the family home, then you should not concede and allow your ex to take the family home. Make sure that you've reflected carefully on your must-haves, and don't make concessions on those issues. But also expect that your ex will likely have their own must-haves.

There is one thing to remember about must-haves, however: the more you both have, the tougher it will be to reach a settlement. Do your best to remain flexible because there is no guarantee that you'll get your must-haves if your negotiations fail and you end up in court.

Deal Maker #5: Avoid retrades

Retrading means backing out of a previous agreement, essentially breaking your word. For the divorce process to work, both you and your ex need to know that when you reach an agreement on an issue you won't have to circle back to revisit it. Once you've agreed on an issue, please don't change your mind. Lead by example and show how you both should follow through on your commitments.

Trust may be in short supply as you head into this negotiation. And maybe you'll never trust each other enough to support an intimate relationship. However, it is possible to build trust within the context of negotiation by making commitments and living up to those commitments. Don't deal with any regret you might feel about certain commitments by backing out of an agreement on an issue. Push harder on the next issue instead.

If your ex tries to retrade, strongly resist, or make them pay dearly. If you allow them to retrade once, the risk is that they'll try this tactic again. You can't develop momentum in the negotiation if it is a constant rhythm of one step forward, two steps back.

Deal Maker #6: Know your bottom line

This sounds like a no-brainer, but it's tougher than it seems. Until you are staring down the barrel of a "take it or leave it" threat from your ex, your bottom line may be hard to pin down, but do make a solid attempt. When you are exhausted by the negotiation, you need to hang on to your resolve and not accept a deal that is below your bottom line. When you are furious and ready for a fight, you don't want to reject an acceptable deal out of spite.

To figure out your bottom line, you need to consider the alternative to reaching an agreement. The alternative is a court-imposed deal. That means your bottom line in the negotiation depends on what might happen if you go to court. You absolutely, positively need the help of your team to figure this out. You'll need your lawyer to educate you on the law, your accountant to translate the law to numbers, and your counselor to help you keep your cool. Unfortunately, it is impossible to precisely determine the best or worst cases in a litigation because everyone in the process, including the judges, is human and the law is subject to interpretation. Still, you need to have a reasonable guess.

If your bottom line in the negotiation is higher than your best possible outcome in court, then I don't like your chances of coming to a deal. Your ex would be crazy to offer you that deal. They'd be better off going to court. Of course, your bottom line shouldn't be below your worst possible outcome in court either. You'd be crazy to take that deal. You'd be better off going to court.

Let's say this is your range of possible outcomes if you go to court:

Your Best

Your Worst

Let's say this is your ex's range of possible outcomes in court:

Ex's Worst

Ex's Best

When we overlap your ranges, we see your "deal zone." That's the sweet spot where, hopefully, you can reach agreement and avoid the courtroom:

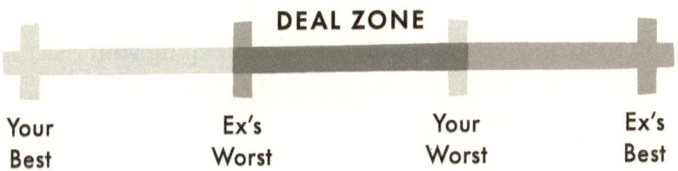

Your bottom line should land somewhere in between the best- and worst-case scenarios you would face if you had to go to court.

To get more specific, your bottom line should not be equal to your best possible outcome in court. Court is uncertain, takes forever, and is expensive and stressful. Your bottom line should be less than your best-case scenario at court because you'll avoid all that crappy stuff if you can negotiate a deal.

Similarly, your bottom line should not be your worst possible outcome in court. Well, I should say that I don't want it to be that low. I mean, what are the odds that you end up with the absolute worst-case scenario at court? Surely, we can do better than that! Let's at least agree that this is the lowest point at which you would put your bottom line.

If you're a risk-taker and you're confident that you can rebuild if things don't go your way in court, then your bottom line should be closer to that courtroom best-case. If you are risk-averse and can't imagine living with the worst-case scenario that the court may impose, then your bottom line should be closer to the courtroom worst-case.

Simply put, set your bottom line based first on your legal rights and responsibilities, and then on your needs, and then on your wants, all the while keeping your risk tolerance in mind. Easy, right? Seriously, I get that it isn't easy. Sorry. You still have to do it.

What we're hoping is that your bottom line and your ex's bottom line create an overlapping deal zone because then you have a shot at a successful negotiation.

By the way, knowing your bottom line doesn't mean you won't fight hard for more. It doesn't mean your team won't fight hard for more. But it's important to know what it is so that you don't reject a good deal or accept a bad deal.

Deal Maker #7: Know your enemy (um, I mean your ex)

What does your ex really care about? It's likely that your ex will care about some things that you don't care much about at all, or they'll value things that you don't value at all. This creates an opportunity to give your ex a concession that is big to them and small to you, and then to push for a concession in return.

Your ex loves the tiny ice-fishing cabin that you built together during the first few years of your marriage. They believe that you love it too. Actually, you would happily never set foot in that smelly, cold place again. In the negotiation, it makes sense to give up the cabin since your ex will highly value that concession and you aren't giving up anything you value.

Pay close attention to your ex's priorities. Don't assume that you know all there is to know about those priorities. People change. Divorce changes people. Pay attention to gain an advantage.

Prepare to Feel Conflicted

Now you are fully prepared to negotiate. I am hopeful that you will be successful. Most people going through divorce avoid court and reach agreement. So I want to be encouraging, but the Pollypragmatist in me also wants you to be prepared, because negotiation won't be easy. And even if you are prepared and embracing your own Pollypragmatist, your ex might not be as enlightened. And even if you are both enlightened and motivated to settle, sometimes the best intentions don't result in a negotiated settlement, so you might have to go through the tough process of litigation. Your personal work, your preparation for negotiation, and your team will all serve you in litigation. (But I'm hoping it doesn't come to that.)

Before we move on to your life after divorce, there's something I need to warn you about. Let's say that you have a successful negotiation and reach a settlement.

```
        Your
       settlement
    _____
     Financial homework
        & negotiation
    _____
   Limbo plan: your secure foundation
    _____
   Healthy thinking & good behavior
```

I didn't draw you on the pyramid this time because, while you might think you will feel like this...

...you might actually feel like this...

... and I want you to be prepared.

Don't be caught off guard if you feel unhappy when you are at your divorce finish line, because that might lead you to misdiagnose the cause of your unhappiness. Let's say that you got your thinking straight, put together a great team, crunched the numbers, engaged in an effective negotiation, and now you're close to finalizing your deal. You can see the end of legal bills in your near future. Yet you're caught off guard by feelings of unhappiness. Where is the elation that you anticipated feeling when all this hell was finally over? If you're caught off guard, then you might conclude that you struck a bad deal and that's why you're unhappy.

OK, yes, it's possible that it's a bad deal. And, yes, it's possible that you shouldn't sign it, that you should walk away and proceed with litigation. But think carefully about that move. You've worked hard to get to this point with the help of a great team. And litigation sucks.

Hopefully, what I'm about to say next may give you some comfort in a strange kind of way. I haven't met one person who felt great about their divorce deal when they signed the final papers. Even a fair financial deal doesn't feel like a win. Nobody gets everything they want. Signing on the dotted line involves abandoning the hope for everything you wanted and accepting what you got. This is not the conclusion of an exciting business deal that inspires champagne and a fancy dinner. This is the conclusion of your marriage. And, on your wedding day, it wasn't the end you had in mind.

I don't like ending this chapter on a sad note. But forewarned is forearmed, and I know that you have the courage to face the truth. On a happier note, in the next chapter I'll meet you on the other side and we'll talk about life after divorce.

> **A Quick Summary**
> - Remember, it's only money.
> - Manage your fear and lower your emotional temperature.
> - Don't move too fast or too slow.
> - Don't lie, cheat, or steal.
> - Make concessions and make them wisely.
> - Don't retrade.
> - Know your bottom line and know your ex.
> - When you reach a settlement, be prepared that you might feel sad and exhausted instead of happy. That doesn't mean it's a bad deal.

8
The Finish Line

The real finish line is realizing you haven't thought about your divorce in a week.

When I started doing divorce work, after my clients successfully reached a settlement we would just high five and I would move on to my next client. But then I noticed that, for many of these clients, completing their divorce didn't mean they were ready to skip merrily into their after-life—I mean their after-divorce-life, of course. The actual afterlife can wait.

There are some things you need to know to be prepared for your postdivorce life. Most of all you'll need a plan and probably some help to successfully transition from divorcing to divorced.

The Aftereffects of Divorce

You might miss your divorce. That sounds super strange, doesn't it? Right now you might be thinking, "There is no bloody way that I will miss my divorce." But you might.

Here's why. Heading into divorce, you probably fantasized about how amazing it will be to emerge out the other side. But it's possible that, once you do emerge, you'll feel like a shriveled husk of your former self with half of your former net worth. You might be disappointed to find that it isn't amazing, it's empty and sad. You may worry that you'll never feel whole and happy. Please know that it's normal to feel empty and sad when your divorcing life stage is over. You aren't weird or alone.

We've probably all experienced the emotional and physical crash that comes when we finish a big project. After we've written our last final exam, or unpacked the last box in our new home, or unwrapped the last gift on Christmas. The crash. Maybe we get sick or tired or sad or all three. It's like the project was our life source and, when it's over, we're drained. Divorce is one of those big projects. And "drained" isn't a big enough word to describe the crash. There is a gaping hole in your life where your divorce lived. You might miss the energy that divorcing provided.

You might also be missing some relationships. When the divorcing is over, sometimes divorce-stage relationships are also over or very much altered. You might be happy to see that last big legal bill, but you might miss your lawyer. In my own practice, my clients and I often get attached. And while I maintain relationships with many former clients, we are no longer in the trenches together and we certainly connect less often. And maybe they miss me like I miss them.

You will also have friends or family members who become your key supporters during your divorce. The intimacy in those relationships is magnified as they help you navigate the tough times. And while they will still be in your life, the relationship will (or should) return to balance. It won't be all about you anymore. No judgment! You needed it to be all about you for a while. Still, while I'm sure you want balanced relationships, you might feel some loss as you return to that balance.

Finally, as shocking as it sounds, you might miss the connection with your ex. It's more common to move from strong positive feelings during marriage to strong negative feelings during divorce. It's less common to move from strong positive feelings to apathy. And strong feelings are a bond. And it hurts to break bonds.

People don't talk about missing their divorce. We probably don't talk about these feelings because missing divorce sounds odd. But it can happen. If it happens to you, acknowledge it, accept it, feel it, and move on. Worse than dealing with the challenge of crossing the divorce finish line is not making it to the finish line at all, and then spending the rest of your life stuck in the divorcing life stage. I really don't want that for you, so here's what to keep in mind.

Moving-On Idea #1: Look to the road ahead

Going through divorce can be like living as a main character in a dramatic movie or maybe a thriller or a horror. It typically involves dramatic turns of events, conflict, and passion. Since divorcing can take years, you run the risk of becoming addicted to the drama.

Beware that pitfall. It leads to hanging on to the conflict of the divorce or finding other events in life to inject with toxicity. You may end up vilifying your ex or finding a new character to cast as villain, like your lawyer who didn't fight hard enough for you, or your boss who takes you for granted, or the grocery clerk who puts your tomatoes at the bottom of the bag.

It is time to shift your perspective to the future and let go of any remaining toxic energy from divorcing. Most likely you will have a new list of divorce-related transgressions for which to blame your ex or shame yourself. Ditch those. Hanging on to that list will keep you stuck in the past, stuck in your divorce, and that's no way to live.

When you go through divorce, it is an extended process of moving *away* from something. Moving away from your marriage, both the relationship and the life. Let's call that "push energy." Successfully moving out of your divorce requires creating "pull energy," creating something that you *want* instead of rejecting something that you *don't want*. Future versus past. Good versus bad.

When you were married, your life was constrained by your relationship and the existence of a shared reality. But maybe the life you created as a result wasn't the exact sort of life that you would have created without constraints. You now have an opportunity to create a life free from those constraints. Embrace that opportunity. Expand your horizons with a new job, new hobby, new puppy, or a hot new love. Something to pull you into your big fat fabulous future.

Don't worry if you aren't sure what your next step will be. Even though I'm not a big fan of being patient or embracing uncertainty, that's often exactly what you need to do to figure out the next big thing when the previous big thing ends. Your marriage is your previous big thing. Give yourself some time to figure out your next big thing. Inspiration will strike if you're open to it.

Moving-On Idea #2: Watch out for postdivorce behavior pitfalls

I feel like such a mom, telling you to be well behaved in your postdivorce life. But I'm saying this for your own good. (OK, now I really feel like a mom.) There are common postdivorce behavior pitfalls that I want you to avoid.

First, there will be things you don't like about your final settlement. You will likely have some legitimate beefs about your ex, or their family, or their behavior. But, please, don't gossip. Gossiping will make it tougher to shift your focus from the yucky past (your divorce) to your bright future. If that isn't reason enough, people will get tired of hearing about your ex. Seriously, it gets boring. When gossip is new, it might be rude but at least it's exciting. When gossip is old news, it's rude and boring, a bad combination. Time to move on for everyone's sake (but mainly yours).

Next, there will be things you don't like about the way your ex is dealing with postdivorce life. Some of those things might even feel like they're your business, like how they interact with your kids or those friends you continue to share, or the mess they leave at the shared family cottage. But, please, don't rant at your ex; your license to rant expired with your marriage. For successful postdivorce relations with your ex, you need to beef up your boundaries with one another. In the same way that you wouldn't rant at the grocery clerk (at least I don't recommend it because the video might go viral), you shouldn't rant at your ex. Sure, you might need to express displeasure now and then. Dust off the book *BIFF* by Bill Eddy and keep it Brief, Informative, Friendly, and Firm.

And you knew this next one was coming, right?

The whole "do what's best for the kids" thing is top of mind for people going through divorce. The topic comes up in every book you read, video you watch, and conversation you have with your counselor. But when your divorce is wrapped up and you settle into your after-life, you run the risk of forgetting this guiding principle. Please don't.

As a stepmom, I made a solemn vow to never, ever trash-talk my stepkids' mom. Like, ever. I'm no saint, but as a kid of divorced parents, I know how it feels to hear even mildly negative stuff about your parents from your parents. It sucks. If your parents remain married, I'm not sure that it sucks in the same way. In fact, when my husband and I tease one another for our various shortcomings, our kids seem delighted. But probably only because they know we love each other. I'm racking my brain, but I can't remember a time when I've broken my vow of no trash-talking and we are coming up on twenty years. But I know this: if I did break my vow, it would stick with my stepkids. If they read this, they'll definitely remember whether or not I broke this vow because this shit matters for the rest of your dang life. Don't forget to do what's best for the kids. Forever.

Moving-On Idea #3: Assemble your post-divorce team

Remember when we talked about the sort of support you will need during your divorce? You'll also want to think about the sort of support you will need during your life after divorce. Your ex handled certain areas of life during your marriage. Depending on the length and nature of your marriage, you may have gotten a bit rusty at dealing with those areas. Time to fill in the gaps in one of three ways:

1. Do it yourself.
2. Hire help.
3. Have your new partner take care of it.

I'm trying to remain open-minded here because I have a strong preference for #1 and #2 and I really hate #3. Just being up front with you.

Here's why I like #1. Learning new skills or brushing up on the rusty ones is empowering. And it also ensures that you are resilient, protected, safe—this is a hot-button for me. My independent, risk-averse nature has been reinforced by my personal and professional experiences with divorce. Intellectually, I think that it's perfectly normal and healthy to depend on others, but I still get uncomfortable at the thought.

During her marriage, my sister wasn't the family financial manager. In her post-divorce life, she became a kick-ass financial manager. She became a poster woman of responsible financial stewardship and in her mid-fifties she reached financial freedom. She's my hero. Although it's hard to imagine now, her transition took some effort. You aren't alone if you feel a wee bit intimidated at the prospect of doing things yourself, but you can do it!

Here's why I like #2. You don't need to be an expert in all things. You don't need to do all things. Marriage meant two people to take care of life's business. Single means twice the workload. So it's reasonable to expect that you're going to need help.

There are also great things about hiring someone else instead of relying on your spouse. First, you'll hire an *expert*. I'm not knocking your ex, but there's a good chance they weren't an expert at handling all of their assigned tasks in your married life. When my computer craps out or the Wi-Fi quits working and I yell for my husband, he assures me that he isn't an IT expert. To which I reply, "Then what am I paying you for?" (Before realizing that I'm not paying him.) Obviously, in the moment, I'm a little worked up because there's no Wi-Fi. You get my point. Hiring someone means getting the right person for the job.

Second, when you hire someone, they have to do what you say. Glory be, I'm in heaven. But seriously, I love the idea that you retain control over the big important stuff in your life. Maybe you aren't all that picky about the way the lawn is mowed or the toilets are scrubbed, but it's good to be picky when it comes to how your money is invested and whether or not you'll run out of cash before you kick the bucket at age 120 after crashing your sports car in the streets of Madrid.

Here's why my least favorite is option #3, the one that involves passing big responsibilities to your new partner. I'm biased against this option as a result of my work and my nature. I don't love the idea of you being reliant on your mate in the big important areas in your life, especially your finances. It feels risky to me. I worry about my kids relying on their partners in this area. I try to keep that worry to myself. But there it is. Now they know. Since it's in a book, maybe they'll listen. On the other hand, I'm their mom, so maybe not. Can you give them a call and warn them please?

Your After-Divorce Finances

Now that you're single, there is some financial stuff that's going to need doing, either by you or someone else.

Money Matter #1: The day-to-day stuff

If you've been separated for a while, odds are this one has already come up. This day-to-day stuff is tough to subcontract out because it's things like paying your bills, managing your grocery costs, figuring out whether you can afford to pay someone to mow your lawn or clean your house, and choosing the right dang points card among the bajillion options.

Your banker can help you get things organized but, beyond that, this is a do-it-yourself area. You'll find efficient ways to handle things, such as automatic or online bill payment, creating a standard grocery list, and choosing one points card so your wallet isn't overflowing (or scanning them to your smart wallet on your smartphone if you're younger than me). And you'll figure out spending patterns that work for you, whether that's hiring the neighbor kid to mow your lawn in exchange for Freezies or hiring someone to clean your toilets while you take care of the vacuuming. Really, the day-to-day stuff isn't as bad as you might imagine. I promise.

Money Matter #2: Planning for the future

Here's hoping that you have a bit of a nest egg from your divorce. But even if you don't, or especially if you don't, you'll need to come up with a plan for your financial future. I get that this one might feel scary. Sometimes ignorance feels blissful when it comes to figuring out whether you'll ever be in a position to retire. But ignorance doesn't help you plan. I believe that when you face the financial facts, you'll do what needs to be done to meet your financial goals. But not if you're ignorant, not if you don't have a plan. So this is one of those areas in which you'll likely need help.

As an accountant, I cringe a bit at the label "financial planner." I've been called a financial planner a few times in my career, and I immediately explain that I'm an accountant, a divorce financial adviser, not a financial planner. Sort of silly, really. I don't think anyone means it as an insult. But here's the issue. There's a wide range of folks who call themselves financial planners. Some are amazing professionals who have loads of expertise and operate entirely in their clients' best interest. But some are sleazy salespeople operating entirely in their own best interest. This is too bad, because it's a vital role.

I want all of my clients to receive solid financial planning, so it's worth sifting through the service providers to find the amazing ones. If you decide to hire a financial planner, consider all those factors we talked about in chapter 4. Find out whether or not they're trying to sell you something. I'm not saying that's an immediate deal-killer. I've met some skilled, reputable salespeople whom I trust to put their clients' interests ahead of the desire for a sale. They understand that selling people stuff they don't need is bad business in the long run. Still, I want you to have your eyes wide open if your financial planner is also looking to sell you, say, life insurance.

Money Matter #3: Financial housekeeping

Now that the monumental project of your divorce is complete and the financial dust has settled, it's time to do some financial housekeeping. Buying life insurance, filing your taxes, drafting your will: this is not sexy or exciting stuff. But life (and death) gets exciting if you don't take care of this stuff, and not in a good way. Taking care of this stuff will make you feel safe, secure, and settled, and the older I get, the sexier those things sound.

So, consider getting professional help. Sure, if your finances are super-duper simple, maybe you can file your own taxes or get a will-drafting package from the local pharmacy. But this gives me those same jitters that the idea of your do-it-yourself divorce plans gave me. Time to ask yourself a few questions before you decide to handle this stuff on your own.

Here's where to start:

1 Do I have the necessary expertise, or am I prepared to invest gobs of time to learn? (Warning: on this question my bias is showing!)

2 Is my situation so incredibly simple that I can't do any serious damage by doing stuff myself that typically would require expert help? (Oops, there it is again.)

3 Do I want the tax authorities at my door or to leave a legacy of mess and struggle for my beneficiaries? (OK, I obviously can't help myself.)

Just hire experts to handle this stuff. Get it done right the first time.

Money Matter #4: Wealth management

That sounds sort of fancy, doesn't it? Wealth management. Sounds like something that's reserved for rich folks. But, actually, wealth management is for everyone, regardless of your wealth. Wealth management is about making your money work for you, whether you have a little or a lot, and that's important for your financial future. It's a rare bird who effectively invests without the help of an expert.

Unfortunately, choosing the right wealth manager isn't easy. It's another sector in which there is a broad range of service providers—from absolute crap to wonderful—so do your due diligence. Just like financial planners, you need to be aware of potential conflicts of interest when hiring a wealth manager. If your wealth manager makes higher fees when you make particular investments, can you trust them to maintain an unbiased perspective? Again, I'm not saying these conflicts are immediate deal-killers. The wealth management business is chock-full of these conflicts and you wouldn't have a ton of options if you insisted on avoiding them altogether. But please choose your adviser carefully and think critically about their recommendations.

Money Matter #5: Getting help when you need it

Even if you loved your lawyer, you're probably going to be delighted when the legal bills stop rolling in. But don't let that prevent you from reaching out if you need more help. Even the best settlement agreements have room for interpretation, or for misinterpretation. Be prepared for the fact that your ex might have a slightly different vision for implementing the support clause or for what "shared decision-making" means when it comes to those assets that you decided to co-own. Just like during your divorce, I don't want litigation to be your first approach to these challenges. Maybe you can resolve the problems directly with your ex. Or maybe you'll need the help of your divorce lawyer to work through bumps in the road as you implement your settlement agreement.

The Real Finish Line

I thought I should get over my divorce. So when I was still occasionally awash with grief, years later, I thought there was something wrong with me. And then I had an epiphany. What I was resisting was persisting; resisting was causing my suffering. For me, healing came from letting go of all that resisting. I accepted that my first marriage and my divorce were part of me and not something to "get over." I let go of the need to justify it, or understand it, or explain it. Now, coming up on two decades later, I'm at peace with it.

I'm guessing this isn't the most uplifting news you've heard. Peace after twenty bloody years?! That's what you're offering?! All right. I can do better than that. I think that healing from divorce comes in layers, fits and starts, waves. I think the healing starts right away. Like the healing from a terrible wound. The scabs and bruises make it seem worse before it seems better, but you're healing. And then you start noticing. Maybe you sleep through the night, don't think about your divorce for a week, or your fifteenth wedding anniversary comes and goes without a thought. Maybe that private joke you shared with your ex crosses your mind and gives you a laugh instead of a cry.

The real finish line sneaks up on you. The real finish line is when you are divorced and no longer divorcing. When divorce is something that happened but not something that defines your present and future. The real finish line is acceptance. It is peace.

You'll make it, love.

xo,
KELLY

Recommended Resources

Books to Support Healthy Thinking

The Four Agreements: A Practical Guide to Personal Freedom by Don Miguel Ruiz
Loving What Is: Four Questions That Can Change Your Life by Byron Katie with Stephen Mitchell
The Power of TED: The Empowerment Dynamic by David Emerald
The Untethered Soul: The Journey Beyond Yourself by Michael Singer

Books to Help You Through Your Divorce

BIFF: Quick Responses to High-Conflict People by Bill Eddy
Conscious Uncoupling: 5 Steps to Living Happily Even After by Katherine Woodward Thomas
The Divorce Survival Guide: The Roadmap for Everything from Divorce Finance to Child Custody produced by Calistoga Press
The New Rules of Divorce by Jacqueline Newman
The Optimist's Guide to Divorce: How to Get Through Your Breakup and Create a New Life You Love by Suzanne Riss and Jill Sockwell

Resources for Marriage, Reconciliation, and Recovery from Infidelity

The Exceptional Seven Percent: The Nine Secrets of The World's Happiest Couples by Gregory Popcak
GoAskSuzie.com
The Seven Principles for Making Marriage Work by John Gottman and Nan Silver

Books I Like and Want to Share with You

Atomic Habits: An Easy & Proven Way to Build Good Habits & Break Bad Ones by James Clear
Everything is Figureoutable: The Real Secret to Lasting Success by Marie Forleo
*Healthy as F*ck: The Habits You Need to Get Lean, Stay Healthy, and Kick Ass at Life* by Oonagh Duncan

About the Author

KELLY LAVALLIE is a CPA, CA, CFDS, and CDFA (a bunch of designations that demonstrate her financial and divorce expertise) whose advisory practice helps women navigate financially complex divorces. As a thought leader in the arena of modern divorce, Kelly calls for a measured and pragmatic approach to reduce the suffering that is often part of the global business of divorce. She augments her persuasive and empathetic vision of "untying the knot" with her personal experience, from growing up in a blended family and navigating her own divorce to becoming a parent in her own blended family. Kelly is based in Vancouver, British Columbia.

Learn More About Untying the Knot

Speaking. Bring *Untying the Knot* to a live audience by booking Kelly for a dynamic conversation on money and intimate relationships.

More Support. To go deeper with the ideas shared here, get the accompanying workbook and explore the Untying the Knot course. One-on-one advising is available through Kelly's website.

Connect with Kelly. Learn more about Kelly's practice at lavallie.ca, and follow along online:

- kelly_lavallie
- Kelly LaVallie
- kellylavallie

Bulk Sales. Need more than one book for an upcoming group event, book club, or as an addition to your company library? Inquire about wholesale options at lavallie.ca.

www.ingramcontent.com/pod-product-compliance
Lightning Source LLC
Chambersburg PA
CBHW020904080526
44589CB00011B/438